Goldtop
Believers

by Vic DaPra
& David Plues

ISBN 978-1-57424-4032-8

CENTERSTREAM®

Design – David Plues – Vic DaPra
Copyright © 2021 CENTERSTREAM Publishing
P.O. Box 17878 Anaheim Hills, CA
www.centerstream-usa.com | centerstrm@aol.com | 714-779-9390
All rights for publication and distribution are reserved.

Les Paul MODEL

Thank You

The special merit award once again goes to
Albert Molinaro who devoted his time and experience
finding many of the rare Goldtops for this issue.
thank you Albert.

Goldtop Believer awards go to
Tom Wilson, Mike Slubowski, Gary Dick, Steve Craw
Gil Hembree, Mike Reeder and Damir Sabolovic.

Burst Believers V was an unexpected addition to the series
with many new photographs of unpublished Bursts
including the surprise fifth "lefty." BB V was also a
thank you to the many supporters, and it was a pleasure to feature
so many readers on the front cover and montage pages.

We had many requests to feature other Les Pauls and decided to
concentrate on the Goldtops from 1952 to 1969. We include
many of the variations which developed during these years.
Goldtops are revered by many players for their superior tone
and build quality – not as pretty as a Burst, but equal in
every other respect.

We hope you enjoy the following pages,
Vic and David

Goldtop
Believers

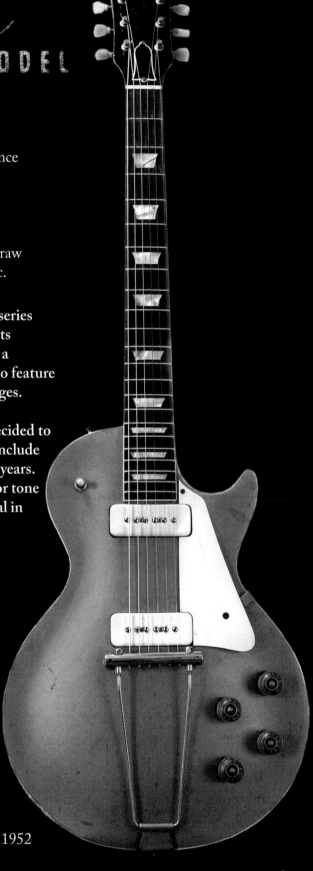

1952

The Les Paul Goldtop
1952 to 1969

It always fills us with pride that so many of you respond so well
to our never-ending requests for help with these books. Once again
your response has been magnificent. With your help, we have
managed to cover the major changes in the Goldtops. The
standard of photography is once again top class and we thank
Ron Middlebrook at Cenerstream for his continued support.

Special thanks to the following people who have helped to make
the book possible:

Bernie Marsden, Eric Clapton, Charlie Daughtry, Slash, Joe Menza,
Elliot Easton, Rick Nielsen, Steve Hackett,
Vince Gill, Joe Bonamassa, Mike Corby, Eliot Michael, Dave Rogers,
Lou Gatanas, Bruce Sandler, Mike Graham, Les Dudek, Clem Clempson,
Tom Wittrock, Brian Ray, Keith Nelson, Eric Hayes, Southpaw Sanctum,
Snowy White, Matt Swanson, Stan Webb, Robert Johnson,
David Gilmour, Eleanor Jane, Richard Thompson, Michael Easton,
Charlie Starr, Geoff Whitehorn, Tom Scholz and Bruce Kulick.

Photo credit: Charlie Daughtry

Rick Nielsen

Rick Nielsen

Photo credit: Mike Graham

I'm a songwriter, musician, performer, guitar lover, and guitar collector with a passion and self-taught both in my playing and my collecting. I just got stuff that I liked if I could afford it or even if I couldn't afford it. I was always looking for, I'm not sure of what or why, maybe catches my eye, or maybe the cool factor? Of course, I know it's gotten out of hand, and believe it or not, I'm trying to thin the herd, but I really still have the intense drive like the kid I used to be. Reading, learning, discovering in hunting for and finding, like when I found my first Gibson Les Paul in 1964, this 1955 Goldtop #5 9940 I found in a used bookstore in Rockford, Illinois and paid $65.00 for it, and still have it today.

GOLDTOP TOP GOLD GOLDTOP

THE GOLDEN YEARS

Starting in 1950, there was a demand for solidbody electric guitars. Fender was well aware of this new craze and produced the Fender Broadcaster which would eventually be named the "Telecaster "Gibson realized they had to jump into this arena or face loss of sales to Fender. Les Paul, a popular guitarist and innovator,had developed "the Log" in the 1940s to avoid getting feedback when playing at higher volumes. Les showed his "Log" guitar with a solid pine center block and glued on sides like a traditional Spanish-style guitar to Gibson, who rejected Les's idea. The "Log" is considered to be one of the first solidbody electric guitars produced. In the next few years to come, Gibson realized they must get on board with the new demand for a solidbody electric guitar.

In 1951, Ted McCarty and his team came up with an idea which The famed eventually would become The Gibson Les Paul Model. There were a few prototypes produced in 1951. Gibson gave Les one of these prototypes for his approval. McCarty had stated that design suggestions with Mr. Paul were limited to the tailpiece and talks of a maple cap over a mahogany body for better clarity and sustain. Les's input to the new model which would bear his name was more cosmetic, for instance, the gold finish. Some models were produced with an all gold finish including the back of the neck and body. The new Les Paul Model had a mahogany body, a one-inch thick maple top, two P-90 single coil pickups, and a trapeze tailpiece with strings fitted under, instead of over a steel bar.

Gibson started production of the new Les Paul Model in 1952. The guitar's first public viewing came in June of 1952 when Les played it at the Paramount Theatre in New York. In early 1953, the new model was given a new improvement. The trapeze tailpiece was discontinued and replaced with a new wrap-around style bridge. This was a major factor in the playability of the guitar and in its sound. It also allowed players an opportunity to hand mute the strings. Also, 1953 saw the addition of the "inked on" serial number, which would last on this model until the end of production in 1960.

Les Paul and Mary Ford

THE GIBSON LES PAUL GUITAR

The famed "Les Paul tones" can now become a reality for all guitar players with this beautiful, solid body Les Paul guitar, incorporating many unusual Gibson features. Striking in appearance with its gold-finished, carved maple top, mahogany body and neck, the Les Paul name is in gold script on the peghead of this model.

A unique, new feature is the metal combination bridge and tailpiece, with the strings making contact on top of the bridge and adjustable both horizontally and vertically. This new style bridge and tailpiece enables the player to dampen the tone with the heel of the picking hand for muffled "Les Paul tones."
* Two pickups have separate tone and volume controls.
* Three position toggle switch activates either or both pickups.
* Tone can be pre-set to any desired quality and change from one pickup to another can be accomplished by a flip of the toggle switch.
* No dead notes - clear, sustaining tones in all positions with the 22 fret finger board.
* No buildup of synthetic tones or feed back.
* Body size - length, 17 1/4", width 12 3/4", scale length, 24 3/4"
* Gibson adjustable Truss Rod neck construction.
* Padded leather strap included.
Les Paul Solid Body Electric Spanish Cutaway Guitar
Case: 535 Faultless

The Les Paul Model would stay the same until mid-1955 when Gibson put the new tune-o-matic bridge and stop tailpiece on the Goldtop. This blockbuster invention is still used today in guitar manufacturing. This model would remain the same until 1957, when the new humbucking pickup was added to the Goldtop. Seth Lover designed the humbucking pickup in 1955, and by 1957 this new innovation was used on many guitars in the Gibson lineup. The humbucking pickup is a huge invention in guitar production and sound. The early humbuckers had a "brushed" cover and no "patent applied for" stickers on the bottom plate. In 1958, the gold finish was replaced in favor of the new cherry sunburst which was used until the end of 1960, when the single cutaway Les Paul Model was discontinued.

Gibson relied on its new SG design to carry them through the advancing rock and roll era. The Firebird series was also a flashy new model. By the mid-1960s, there was a growing demand for Gibson Les Pauls. Guitarists Eric Clapton, Mike Bloomfield and Keith Richards were all playing Les Paul Model guitars. In 1968 Gibson reintroduced the Les Paul Standard (as it was called in the catalog) because of public demand. This model would have the gold finish and two P-90 pickups and remain in the line until late 1969/early 1970 when it was renamed the Les Paul Deluxe. The new Deluxe was fitted with mini humbucking pickups.

This book is dedicated to the Gibson Les Paul Goldtop model
manufactured from 1952 to 1969

The Aces, circa early 1950s. (left to right):
Eugene Lyons, Dave Myers, Junior Wells, Louis Myers.
Courtesy Dave Myers

7

Slash with one of his 1957 Les Paul Standards

SLASH talks Goldtops

"I fell in love with the 1957 Goldtop back in 1990 and have been using it ever since. I have found that the 1957 model generally has a certain weighty tone and smoothness that is unique to them.
I also use a Gibson 1957 reissue Goldtop which sounds great. I recently worked with Gibson to release a Slash model dark-back 57 reissue Goldtop Les Paul called 'Victoria' that is modeled after an original 1957 Goldtop with my particular specs and hardware. I love the 1956 Goldtops with soap bar pickups as well.
Goldtops in general have a great sound that is particular to them."

Above: Gibson's recently introduced Slash "Victoria" Les Paul Standard Goldtop.
Carrying the torch, Slash continues to pay homage to Gibsons' Goldtop legacy with a new model.

Slash with a New Gibson "Victoria" Les Paul Standard Goldtop.

Photos and Feature by Albert Molinaro

Goldtop
Believers

LES DUDEK

SAY NO MORE

MUDDY WATERS

11

When authoring "Believer" books it is an honour when celebrated guitarists agree to take part in the process. Eric took time out to give us this insight regarding Freddie King and the influence he made during these historic formative years. He also supported us when writing Burst Believers IV, and we give special thanks to him for this and all he has done for the world of music.

A significant event for me was when a friend brought out a record by Freddie King, an instrumental called "Hideaway." I never heard Freddie King before, but when I listened to it, it simply blew my mind. On the B side of "Hideaway" was "I Love The Woman" which had a guitar solo in the middle which took my breath away. He had a unique kind of playing in which he bent the strings and produced sounds that gave me the shivers. It was like a new light for me to move towards.

Eric Clapton

Eric would use many Gibson guitars during the '60s - 335's SG's Firebirds and Bursts - none more famous than the Beano Burst. The sound of powerful pickups overdriving British amplifiers during this era was an integral part of his playing and sound. As amplification and P.A. systems became more sophisticated, he would turn to the tone emanating from single-coil pickups.

Thanks to Michael Easton at MESL who assisted with this feature

Eric Clapton playing a '53 to '55 Les Paul Goldtop
Hunter College NYC March 29, 1968.

Eric was seen using this guitar only on one occasion – with Cream, during the second set at Hunter College NYC. The guitar is most likely a 1953-1955 Goldtop – the "stop, tune-o-matic" combination was introduced in the mid part of '55 on this model.

Thanks to Dan – www.groundguitar.com

1952 (early) with some unique features

Close up of the silk-screened Model Name.

The inlaid Gibson logo was positioned lower until 1957, and the tuner bushings were hexagaonal then.

Thanks to Albert Molinaro for these great detailed historical photos of this very early 1952 Les Paul Goldtop together with the specs.

Early guitars did not have a Rhythm / Treble ring. You can also see the "unbound" neck which looks out of place on a Standard Les Paul.

The bridge pickup on early production guitars had off-set mounting screws.

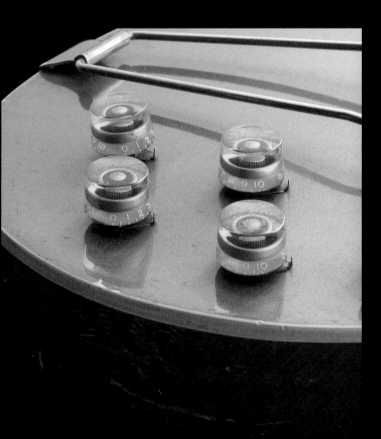

The early Goldtop's had taller, chunky knobs which changed to shorter knobs soon after.

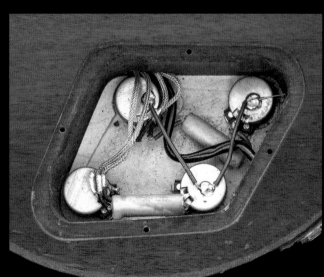

View of the early 1950's control cavity which changed as time went on. It's easy to spot the "maple" top. The IRC Pots date to the 18th week of 1952 on this early guitar.

1952

A very early '52 with the unbound neck and diagonal screws on the bridge pickup

Keith Nelson

Producer/Songwriter/Guitarist and BuckCherry founding member

When I discovered music, guitars and rock 'n roll, I somehow got hip to who inspired my idols of the current day. There would be no Jimmy Page, Keith Richards, Paul Kossoff or Billy Gibbons without Muddy Waters, Freddie King, John Lee Hooker or Hubert Sumlin. While they all are better known for other guitars, all can be seen at some point with an early '50s Gibson Les Paul Standard equipped with P-90 pickups and that majestic gold paint. My teenage brain reasoned that there must be something to it...if it was good enough for them, certainly it would be good enough for me. Not long after, I got my first Gibson electric guitar, which happened to be a Les Paul Standard, that also happened to have that majestic gold paint on the top. Maybe not exactly the early '50s specimen I had hoped for, but I reasoned a 1971 in 1989 was a good start. I've had a few guitars over the years, but my 1952 Goldtop is special to me. Nothing else feels or looks like it. It's usable art, an antique that's relevant today, and most important to me, nothing else sounds like it. Many guitars come and go, but the Goldtop stays!

Keith Nelson

Photo by Albert Molinaro

1952
Bernie Marsden

My good friend Jim Singleton found this one for me – look closely on the scratchplate and you'll see "Les Paul" carved in using a nail.

Jim was with the late Danny Gatton and asked Les Paul to sign it. Les pulled a small nail from his pocket and signed the scratchpate with it, telling Danny and Jim that if they saw a Les Paul signed like this, it was more than likely a genuine Les Paul signature – he didn't like sharpies, it seems!

Thanks to Bernie for allowing this quote to be extracted from his book
"Tales of Tone and Volume" www.rufuspublications.com

1952
All gold model

Photo credit: Tim Matyas

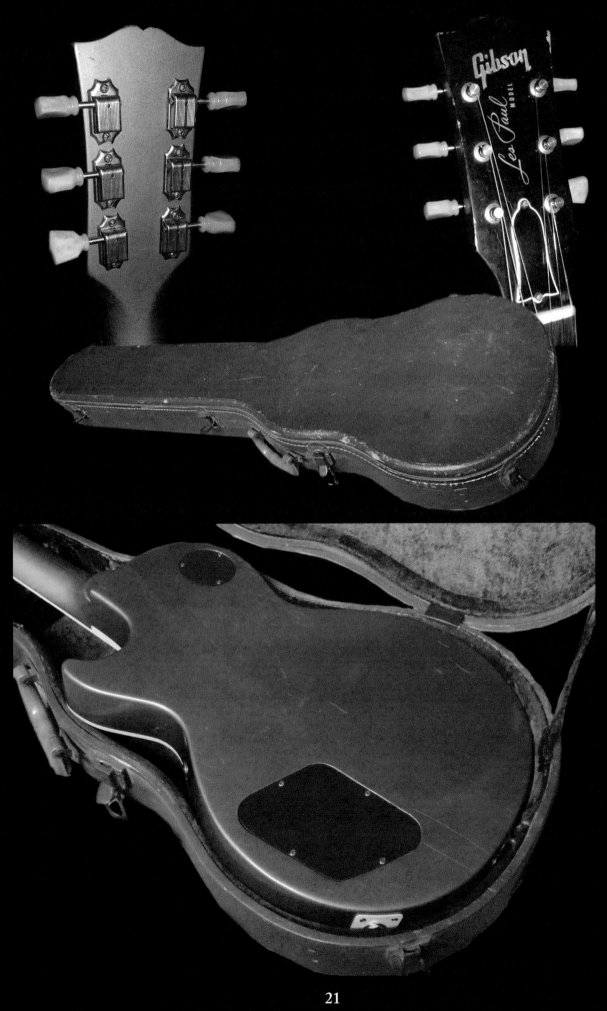

1952 "The Red Devil"

This is probably one of the first modified Goldtops. It was used in "The Song Remains the Same."

An amazing lineup of Jimmy's guitars

Getty image

Mike Corby of The Babys purchased the guitar in 1973 from Maurice Placquet. The Babys had just received a million-pound contract and were looking for equipment. Maurice's Shepherds Bush store specialised in hiring, rehearsals and the sale of Ampeg amps. Mike King, the store manager, lifted the 1952 modified Les Paul from under the counter telling Mike "this is the one." Says Mike, "I was astonished at the natural compression that produced such a fabulous woman tone and sustain."

It had already been refinished red by Dick Knight and a pair of humbuckers installed. The holes from the trapeze tailpiece could still be seen. Mike had seen Mick Taylor performing with the Bluesbreakers and fallen in love with the tone of the Les Paul. He purchased the guitar for £275, a considerable amount at that time, without a haggle.

Mike was invited to bring his triple black Les Paul Custom to the Led Zep rehearsals in Fulham. Jimmy was searching for a replacement for his stolen Black Beauty. Mike also took the Red Devil, in the hope of a "jam." Jimmy eventually purchased the guitar for the previously unheard of sum of £1,000. The full story is told in Burst Believers III.

Thanks to Mike Corby for this feature.

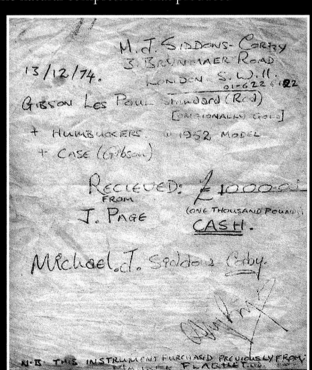

23

1952

Photo credit: Billy Dean

Photo credit: Mike Slubowski

Courtesy Doug and Pat

Courtesy Mike Reeder

Courtesy Mike Reeder

This guitar came from eastern Ontario, Canada, and the original owner bought it in 1952 when he came home from the army. He bought the guitar because he couldn't find work and he used the Goldtop to feed his family in the '50s and '60s.

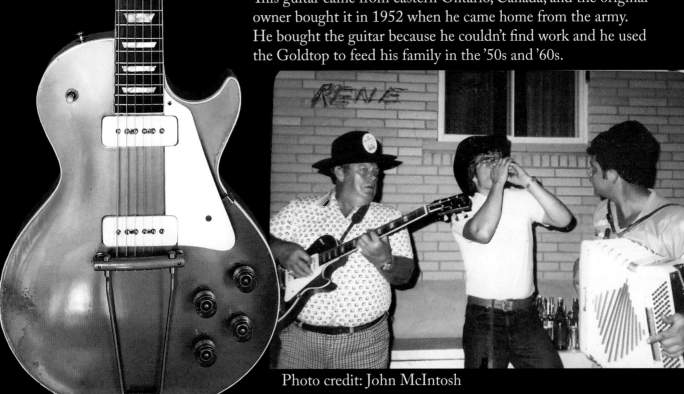

Photo credit: John McIntosh

Carl Perkins

The "King Of Rockabilly" and an early Goldtop player

Carl Perkins was a singer/songwriter who recorded most notably at the Sun Studio in Memphis, in 1954. Some of his best-known songs include his number one hit Blue Suede Shoes, Matchbox, Honey Don't and Everybody's Trying To Be My Baby. Charlie Daniels said, "Carl Perkins' songs personified the rockabilly era." Perkins songs were recorded by such artists as Elvis Presley, The Beatles, Jimi Hendrix, Johnny Cash and Eric Clapton. Paul McCartney claimed that.......
"If there were no Carl Perkins, there would be no Beatles."

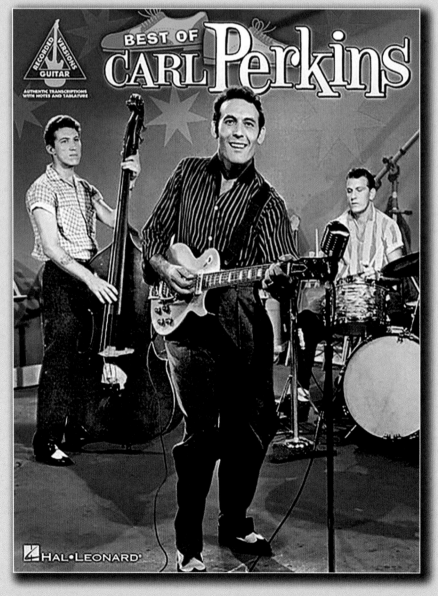

Perkins was born near Tiptonville, Tennessee. He grew up listening to Southern Gospel music. On Saturday nights Carl would listen to the Grand Ole Opry on his Dad's radio. Roy Acuff's broadcasts inspired him to ask his parent's for a guitar. His Dad bought him his first real guitar from a neighbour, a dented and scratched Gene Autry Model. Perkins learned more about guitar playing from John Westbrook, an African-American field worker. Westbrook advised Carl to, "get down close to it, so you can feel it travel down the strings, come through your head and down to your soul where you live."

Commenting on Perkins playing, Sam Phillips has been quoted saying, "I knew Carl could rock and in fact, he told me right from the start that he had been playing that music before Elvis came out on record." Carl Perkins wrote Blue Suede Shoes in 1955 after seeing a dancer get upset with his date for scuffing his shoes. In May of 1964, Perkins toured Britain with Chuck Berry. The Animals backed the performers. On the last night of the tour, Perkins went to a party where the Beatles were in attendance. Ringo asked him if he could record "Honey Don't." Perkins replied, "Man, Go ahead, Have at it." As a guitarist, Perkins used fingerpicking, right-handed damping of the strings along with the use of open strings and single and double string bending. He also used country and blues licks in his songs. In the early years, Carl was seen playing a 1952 or 1953 Les Paul Model.

Called the "King Of Rockabilly", Carl Perkins was inducted into the Rock and Roll Hall Of Fame in 1987.

David Gilmour

3 0148

David Gilmour auctioned 127 of his guitars including these two Goldtops. This '53 sold for $250,000. He is known to prefer the single coil pickup sound and these P-90s graced many Pink Floyd tracks.

5 8225

David Gilmour is famed for his tasteful use of the Fender Stratocaster but he used the '55 Goldtop to record one of his most notable songs, Another Brick in the Wall, (Part 2). He bought the guitar in about '78, because he wanted a Les Paul with P-90 pickups, preferring them to humbuckers. The famous solo was recorded direct to the desk and then played back through an amplifier with added EQ. The guitar sold for $447,000.

1953 and the serial numbets start to appear. Still with the trapeze tailpiece.

A great example from RumbleSeatMusic

Pre and post the Les Paul Goldtop

The hollow body ES 295 was introduced in May of 1952 as a counterpart to the new solidbody Les Paul Model. Some of the early ES 295's had Les Paul's name on the tailpiece. The new solidbody Les Paul Model was debuted in June of 1952 by Gibson with Les playing it at gig in New York City at The Waldorf just a month after the ES 295 was officially released. As you can see the wrap around tailpiece on the 295 with strings over the top would have been nice if used on the cumbersome tailpiece with strings going under on the new Les Paul Model. By mid 1953 Gibson realized the bridge on the Les Paul wasn't accepted well by the players and changed it to a much better wrap around stop bar. The goldtop went through many changes in it's six year existence. By mid 1958 Gibson had taken all the new features of this model and put a sunburst finish on it.

3 0602

Thanks to Dave Rogers and Tim Mullally

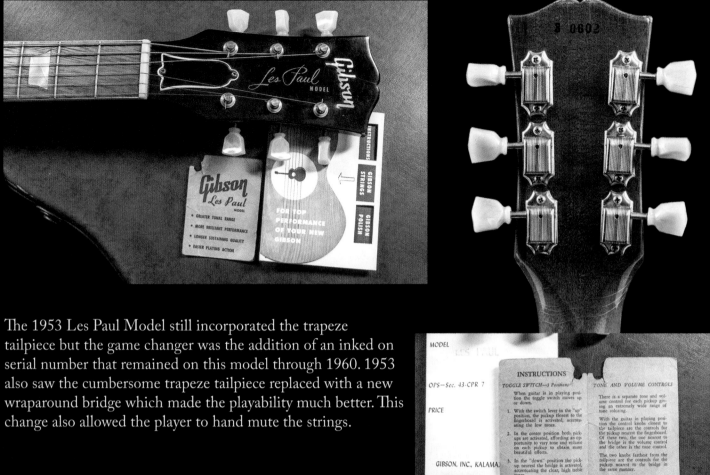

The 1953 Les Paul Model still incorporated the trapeze tailpiece but the game changer was the addition of an inked on serial number that remained on this model through 1960. 1953 also saw the cumbersome trapeze tailpiece replaced with a new wraparound bridge which made the playability much better. This change also allowed the player to hand mute the strings.

Bruce Kulick

3 1202

Photo credit: Neal Zlozower

My '53 Conversion LP Story

My late brother Bob, knew the LP's were important for one's guitar collection. He saw a converted Goldtop on 48th Street at We Buy, that had one double white PAF, a not very professional SB finish, and a mixture of parts. But it was in the mid '70s, so the price was fair and a deal was made. (It included him trading in a 1960 SG/LP).

He used it with Paul Stanley in the studio for Paul's solo LP in 1978. Paul being a big vintage guy loved all the vintage Gibson's as part of the arsenal. Years later with BC Rich making modern rock guitars, and soon to be popular, Floyd Rose instruments to dominate the guitar world, Bob fell out of favor with the old LP. In 1987, he thought of selling it. I told him I would buy the guitar, and it stayed in the family. But everything obsessive I can be about guitars that my brother wasn't into, was about to begin. Paul knew the instrument, and he told me, "get Tom Murphy to paint it right." Done! I continued to replace some of the mixed parts like the tune-o-matic and stop bridge. I found a black PAF pickup for the neck position. Tom got vintage style tulip tuners on the guitar, and the finish was super attractive. It was re-fretted with medium height frets by a Long Island repairman named Joe Pichkur. The inlays were fragile but he pieced any issues together in a beautiful way.

Sound-wise, it's a super guitar. Sweet tone, mojo for days. Leads can be heard on KISS tracks like "Carr Jam", rhythm's on the hit "Forever" and it's been featured on many of my solo CDs. When Vintage Guitar made it the December poster child, I was thrilled It appeared along with other instruments from my collection on the cover of April 2010 for VG. I posed with it many times, but the real joy of owning it, is the fact that is a true Rock 'n Roll tool with all the tone and beauty one would want from a LP. The fact it started as a Goldtop, and some things are not "period perfect" for a conversion is not important. Any guitarist who has played it, knows, it's an amazing testament to the Golden Age of Gibson and my favorite instrument in my collection.

Bruce Kulick (July 2020)

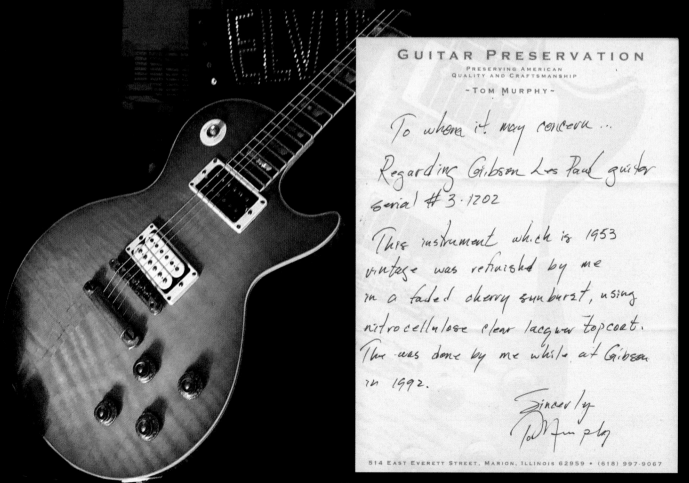

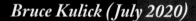

39

The Trapeze construction is an add-on to the original Trapeze which can just be slid on or off. There is a significant improvement to the guitars playability with no alteration to the tone.

Photo credit: Damir Sabolovic

3 1651

Always great to feature leftie guitars and this lovely looking '53 is courtesy of Mrs Jimmy Wallace.

The Southpaw Sanctum

3 1829

Light weight – fat neck
with slight V

3 2003

Photo credit: Tim Errington

Photo credit: Mike Reeder

Photo credit: Jan Malmgren

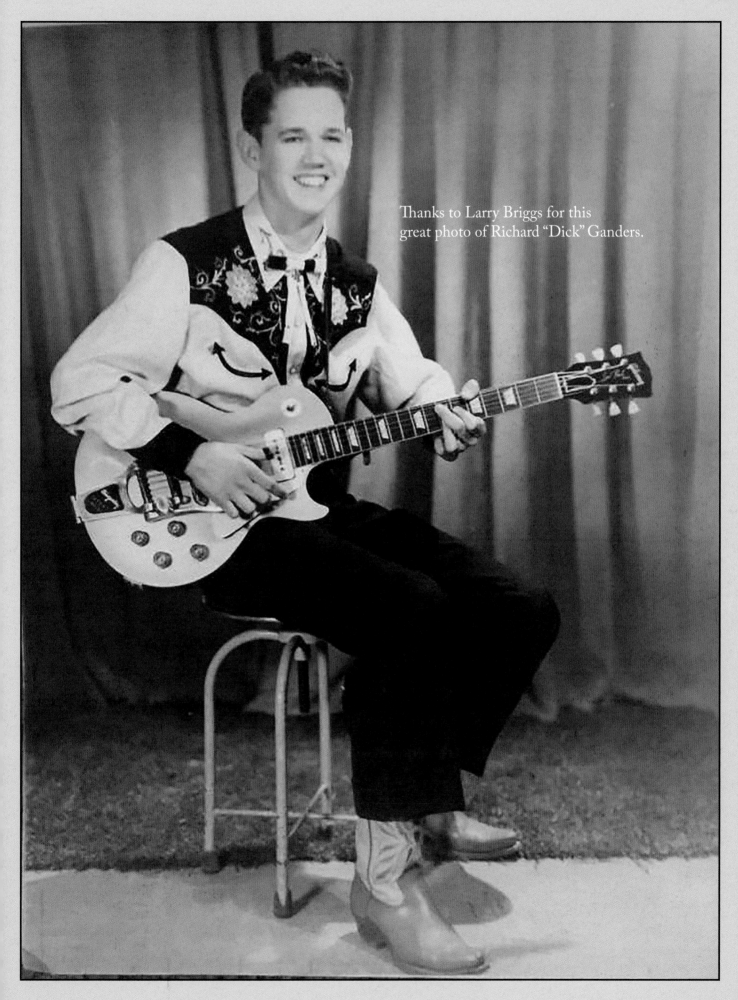

Thanks to Larry Briggs for this
great photo of Richard "Dick" Ganders.

Thanks to Reinhard Berkau

3 2309

Photo credit: Damir Slabolovic

Courtesy of Mike Reeder

3 2779

Photo credit: Dave Peterson

The World's Most Famous Conversion
the '54 Oxblood

Jeff Beck's career started with him stepping into very big shoes in The Yardbirds as Eric Clapton's replacement, then in 1967 splitting off to form The Jeff Beck Group with Ron Wood and Rod Stewart. The early '70s would see Jeff was forging his reputation as a solo artist and one of the hottest guitarists of his generation, and he was doing it on a Gibson Les Paul. The '54 Oxblood LP would find its way to his hands while recording in Memphis and taking time out to visit Strings and Things. He purchased the modified Les Paul from the store, playing it extensively on tour and in the studio. He even gave it pride of place on the cover shot of his milestone 1975 album, Blow By Blow. A tone legend was born.

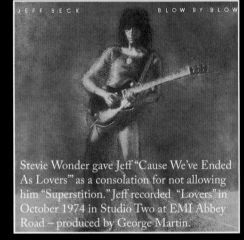

Stevie Wonder gave Jeff "Cause We've Ended As Lovers'" as a consolation for not allowing him "Superstition." Jeff recorded "Lovers" in October 1974 in Studio Two at EMI Abbey Road – produced by George Martin.

We are fortunate to have Burst Believer fan Robert Johnson (RJ), who formerly owned and created the '54 Oxblood LP to provide details. (See Burst Believers IV for more of Roberts spectacular Burst history.)

The 54 Oxblood was my guitar originally. I got it in 1970 from a high school friend's father that bought it new at O.K. Houck music store on Union Avenue. You remember me talking about this great music store. I bought it for $125. I took it to TK who ran the guitar shop in the original Strings and Things music store on Cooper Street to get refinished and install 2 P.A.F.'s I took out of a 1958 ES 335. I had a pair of mint 1960's penny loafer shoes that were oxblood in color and took one of the shoes to TK and told him to paint the guitar this color. TK also took out the small frets and re-fretted the guitar. Later on when Jeff Beck was recording in Memphis at TMI Studio in January of 1972, Beck ended up with the guitar. I was working at TMI Studio as a tape operator with engineer Ronnie Capone on the Beck sessions and part-time session guitarist. TMI Studio was owned by Steve Cropper whom I have known since 1962, as he was a close friend of my Uncle Barry Johnson who was a drummer and went to school with Steve Cropper and Duck Dunn. (continued)

TK & RJ with the '50s shoe the guitar was color matched from

We were hanging around a lot then as there was quite the buzz going on about the Beck recording sessions. Beck also ended up with my 1966 Lake Placid Blue Stratocaster which had a red star inlayed in the body and a P-90 installed in the bridge pickup. I had four Sunbursts at the time, so I was not partial to the Oxblood 54. It was a lot of fun hanging out with Max Middleton, Cozy Powell and Bobby Tench (who I am still friends with), just spent time with Bobby Tench last September. I also played on the Topper Headen solo album with Bobby Tench in 1986."
– RJ

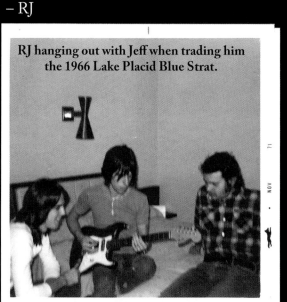

RJ hanging out with Jeff when trading him the 1966 Lake Placid Blue Strat.

This '54 Oxblood LP is probably the most significant modified Goldtop in history – the association with Jeff Beck and Blow by Blow combined to have a dramatic effect on guitarists worldwide. Long meandering solos which had surfaced in the early '70s were finished. Jeff had created with George Martin a new standard of music, technique and guitar excellence. The re-issue from Gibson was a landmark reflecting the skill of the company and the craftsmen involved.

Thanks to Robert Johnson and Tom Keckler at TK's Guitar Services for help with this feature

Photography: Damir Slabolovic

Mike Bloomfield
with his 1954 Goldtop

Mike Bloomfield brought the popularity of Les Paul guitars to new heights in the mid 1960s. He played a 1954 Goldtop with The Paul Butterfield Blues Band.

Mike was one of the first popular music superstars who got his reputation as an instrumentalist. He rarely sang before 1969 and gained his reputation with his music prowess. Mike was inducted into the Blues Hall Of Fame in 2012 and the Rock and Roll Hall of fame in 2015. The price of Goldtops shot up overnight in the mid 1960s when Mike was seen playing his 1954 Goldtop which he later traded to Dan Erlewine and one hundred dollars for Dan's burst. The rest his music history.

Eric Clapton playing the Mike Bloomfield burst, backstage at the Robertson Gymnasium, Santa Barbara, CA. 1968. Thanks to Michael for sharing this great pic with us.
photo supplied by Ed Caraeff.

4 0696

4 1134

This exceptionally fine example has a very rare stinger on the back of the headstock. It seems the wrap around tailpiece has been replaced.

Photo credit: Peter Kriemler

Thin wrap around bridges are common on 1953 to 1955 Goldtops. Note: Kluson deluxe wasn't on the back of tuner at this time.

Note where the Gibson logo is placed – the logo remained in this position until late 1957 when it was moved higher on the headstock, similar to a Burst.

The jackplate showing the squared off type used on 1952 to 1958 Goldtops.

4 1653

Elliot Easton

I used to have a '54 Goldtop with a Leo Quan, that believe it or not, I got from Bun E Carlos (Cheap Trick) with Rick Nielsen approving the deal and inspecting the guitar. I was trading to Bun E a lefty '61 Strat in Candy Apple Red with matching headstock. I used that '54 in concert with The Cars.

It was a great guitar and I played it a lot.

Elliot

Thanks to Elliot for this feature and Steve Craw who provided the photo of 4 1698

4 1726 'Lucky'

Formerly owned by the late
Terry Morgan

Thanks to Danny Boucher
– Premier Music Services
and Ricky Steel Edge

4 1748

This particular '54 shows an angle where the face is a beautiful gold color and the bottom image shows this Les Paul in a different setting showing the extensive lacquer checking and an incredible wide flame top seen through the finish.

Thanks to Marco Berger

69

4 2160

I came across a fantastic '54 a few
minutes away from home. It ticked
all my boxes; wraptail, original – plays
and sounds wonderful.
Eirik

Photo credit: Eirik Jaer

4 2446

4 3427

A museum piece all gold 1954 Goldtop

Thanks to Dave Rogers
and Tim Mullally

Mini Les Paul's 1955,
prototype # 1 and # 2

Photo credit: Tom Harrison

4 3684

4 3979

Freddie King (1934 1976) – part one

Blues and rock guitarist and singer. One of "the Three Kings" of electric blues guitar along with Albert King and B.B. King.

The Freddie King style was developed from the Delta blues and the hard-edged Chicago blues. He moved from Texas to the south side of Chicago. Learning to play in 1949 he would sneak into the local clubs soaking in the blues music. His use of Gibson guitars, particularly the Goldop and '345 became his trademark sound. Freddie was listening to the music of Muddy Waters, Howlin' Wolf, T-Bone Walker, Elmore James, and Sonny Boy Williamson. He would eventually play and learn his craft with Muddy Waters' band members. With hits including "Have You Ever Loved A Woman" (1960) "Hide Away" (1961). Albums such as Let's Hide Away and Dance Away with Freddy King (1961) he was now a major player.

New young players coming on the scene such as Jerry Garcia, Dickey Betts and Stevie Ray Vaughan were all taking in the technique of Freddie and developing their own particular style. In the UK, Eric Clapton, Peter Green, Jimmy Page, Chicken Shack and The Rolling Stones were all emulating his style The John Mayall Bluesbreaker LP with Eric Clapton featuring Hide Away would catapult public awareness of Freddie's great talent and spawn a whole new generation of music and musicians. His legacy is still felt and appreciated today.

Freddie's recording career was not an easy one – in the 50s he had competition from BB King, Muddy Watters and Howlin' Wolf – Chess records were not interested in recording him. Chicago was known for its two main music centres – the established South Side and newer West Side. Freddie would dominate the West Side. 1959 was the career-changing year for Freddie when he was signed to King Records and in 1960 recorded have 'You Ever Loved a Woman'. On the same session, he would record 'Hide Away' which was a major hit, unusual for the period being an instrumental. This instrumental trend would follow with the 'staple' musicians guitar piece 'The Stumble'. Jeff Beck would feature this song on the 1998 'Beckolgy' 3 CD album plus a cameo appearance performing part of the song in the film 'Twins'.

Billy Gibbons and Dusty Hill

"We came to pay tribute to Freddie on a number of levels and a number of reasons," he says. "We have a long standing history of, first of all, loving the music he was doing, and later, the surprise was getting to be friends and having him mentor and teach us a few things."

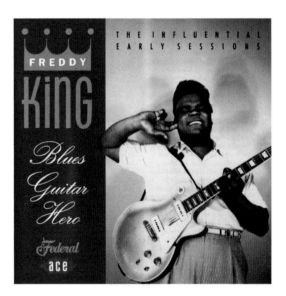

In 1967 Freddie had his first international tour in the UK. This was followed followed by signing to Atlantic Records in 1968 which resulted in two LPs, Freddie King Is a Blues Master (1969) and My Feeling for the Blues (1970), in 1969 he appeared at the Texas Pop Festival alongside Led Zeppelin. He was now star status.

Until his death in 1976 Freddie was touring almost full time and paid little heed to his health. A poor diet and liking for alcohol would see this great musician die at the young age of 42. He was a truly inspirational influence on so many artists leading the field with the use of his Gibson Les Paul Goldtop and revolutionary electric blues technique.

Freddie King (1934 1976) – part two
The UK tours 1967 1969

There is no doubt of the role Freddie King played in the music world and especially the influence he had on guitarists This blues-rock player did not compromise with his style. He plugged his guitar in and cranked it 'all the way up'. He had everything tone, sustain and technique. His riffs and use of string bending and vibrato were exceptional.

Eric is on record as saying "Freddie King, that was serious, proper guitar playing and I haven't changed my mind ever since. I still listen to him and I get the same boost now that I did then."

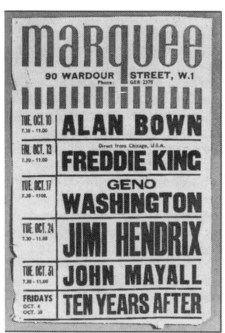

Freddie along with Howlin Wolf and Muddy Waters would make the journey across the Atlantic and perform in the Blues clubs around the UK.

Stan Web recalls his experience working with Freddie

Freddies first tour in 1967-68 was organised by promoters Rick and John Gunnell. Chicken Shack, including Christine Perfect and Andy Sylvester, were booked to support him and work as his band – When they met up he just told them "just join in with me man." He liked my style of playing and there was a lot of mutual respect. I was disappointed he was using a stereo '345 and not his Goldtop. He didn't have the tone of his earlier LP's such as 'Sings', but his playing was inspirational. An imposing guy to be around also a great motor mechanic who ended up repairing our J2 Comma van at the side of the M4.

We were s rehearsing at the Ramjam Club and performing gigs including the Queen Elizabeth College, Manor House and 100 Club (with Georgie Fame). The most memorable concert was the Saddle Theatre (owned by Brian Epstein) with fellow artists John Mayall, Fleetwood Mac (John MacVie would meet and marry Christine after this one) and Howlin' Wolf. Also performing was Stevie Wonder who was now in the superstar league but here he was just another artist. In the audience were Keith Richards and Mick Jagger. A truly amazing gig. We all went to the 'Speekese' afterwards and Stan asked Mike Veron what he should call Howlin' Wolf – the answer, "just Wolf." I asked him what he was drinking, bought him a whisky then the Wolf simply turned and went on his way without so much as a thanks.

David Illingworth reviewed the King/Chicken Shack gig Nag's Head Battersea Nov. 1967
The year's most significant concert was the under publicised 17 date tour by Freddie King which drew thousands of fans who knew him by reputation and as an important influence. Martin Newman who also reviewed **the events remarked the audience was visibly and audibly moved "Freddie King is one of the best of the younger blues artists and certainly the most exciting to visit Britain for some time."**

Freddie would return to the UK in 1969 with the Steam Hammer tour. The Killing Floor was supporting at the Klooks Keek, West Hampstead. Freddie came straight to a short band rehearsal from his flight from Dallas, amazingly patient and polite after a rigorous journey. We ran through the beginnings of "Hideaway", "Have you ever Loved a Woman" etc, and also played the great "Someday after a while" – the only time we ever played it together. Afterwards, Freddie took us over the road to a Wimpy bar and bought us each a hamburger. "Ah", said Lou, quoting a BB King song, "he's paying the cost to be the boss!" He returned for two more tours when we backed him.

Playing with Freddie was a great experience. He was totally professional and self-assured on stage, and would simply shout a key. "E!" and count us in "1, 2, 3. 4." and off we'd go, never quite sure which song we were about to play. Then he'd stop the band with a wave of his guitar while he went into solo guitar, walkabouts around the stage, always smiling and holding the audience's attention. A real pro.

Freddie King with Killing Floor at the L.S.E. London, 1969
Bazz Smith, drums, Paul Taylor, bass Mick Clarke, (guitar) Lou Martin (keys) (ex Rory Gallagher)

Extract from Dunstable Gazette 6 June 1969
Freddie King and Killing Floor tore the house apart. Then the King came on. Right from the first number, he had the audience in the palm of his hand. He tortured his guitar into producing sounds I didn't think were capable of coming from strings. Killing Floor toned right down while backing him Freddie came over with great clarity. The first half had been incredible, but it was nothing to what was to come in Freddie's second set. His guitar work was so superb that it made Clapton's look like the first lesson in the Bert Weedon Guitar Primer.

A message to Mick Clarke from Freddies daughter
I am Freddie's daughter and I really appreciate your email the photos and story. I remember when my father returned from Europe with one of Killing Floor's album. Now after all these years I now know the story behind the album.
Thanks again *Wanda King*.

We are indebted to Stan Webb and Mick Clarke for help with this feature.

Alan Wilson
Canned Heat

The late Alan Wilson with his heavily modified
1954 Goldtop. The guitar featured at the
Monterey International Pop Music Festival 1967,
Woodstock 1969 and The Texas International
Pop Festival, 1969. It was typical of this era,
that the guitar was chosen for its great sound
and that the appearance was of little concern.

Thanks to Tom Wittrock and the
Les Paul Forum for help with this feature.

The Goldtop lefties
by Steve Craw

1953   4 3389   (all gold),   4 1698

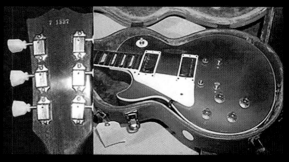

The original owner was Jack Reid who scrapped the original pickguard for one that he had his named engraved into. Gil Hembree had a replacement made, removed the Bigsby and sold it to John MacEnroe.

Formerly Norm Harris

1952

1957 with p90s. formerly owned by
Cesar Rojas of Los Lobos.

1952

1954

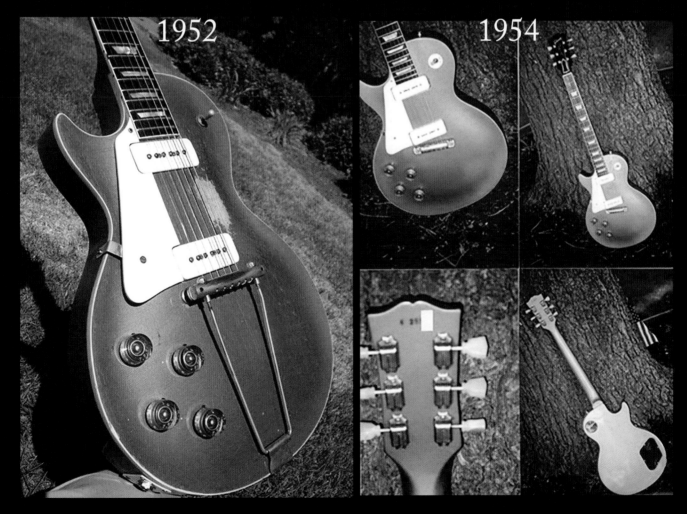

5 6665

Courtesy Mike Reeder

Music Center,
841-1521.
GUITAR- Gibson, Les Pau
and amplifier, $200 com
423-9812.
MMOND ORGAN-US

Paul Drennan story
(bassist for Vince Neil & George Lynch)

Paul purchased this '55, together with a small amp, in 1969 from a lady in Orlando whose husband had passed
away. $200 was a hefty price in those days and he offered all he could – $150. In the late 70s, he traded it to
Tony Battaglia for a Strat. The guitar was used on top 10 hit song Thunder Island by Jay Ferguson in 1977.
Over the years he tried to re-purchase the guitar with no success but in 2013 Tony contacted him offering to
sell. The deal went ahead and Paul was reunited with the guitar which he claims still smells the same as when
he first opened the case in Orlando, back in 1969. Paul is currently playing guitar with blues band
Three Forks Road.   Thanks to Paul Drennan

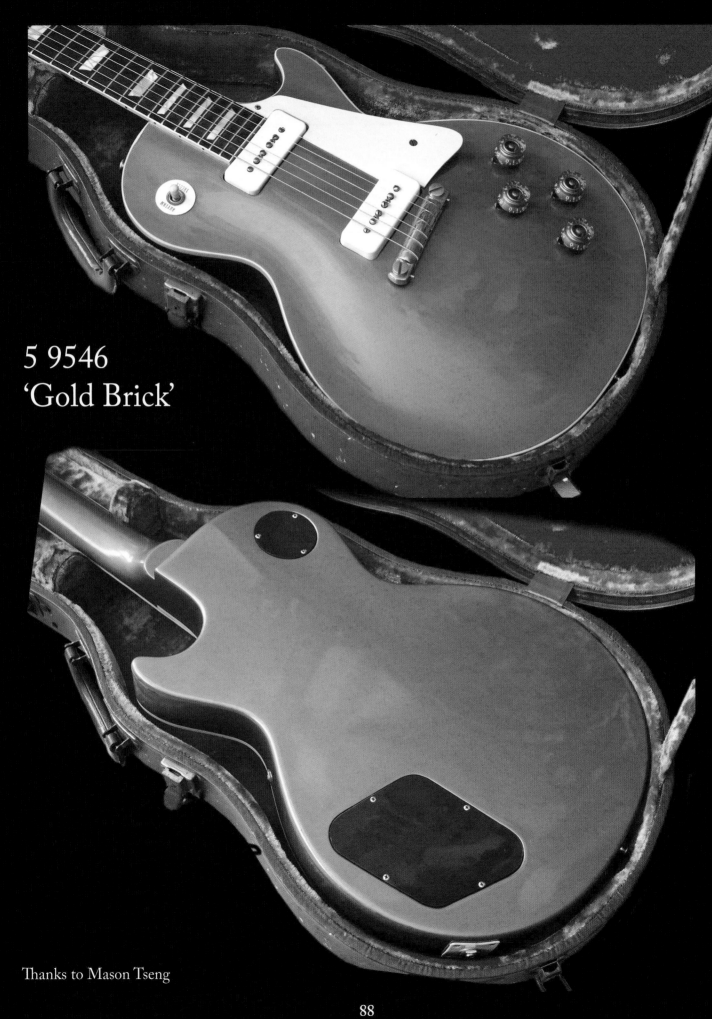

5 9546
'Gold Brick'

Thanks to Mason Tseng

5 9553

Photo credit: Andy Cesarini

5 9940 Rick Nielsen

Goldtop Believer – from one of the most iconic players, collector and loveable characters in the guitar world – the amazing Rick Nielsen who still loves to get out there performing and thrilling us with the sound of the Les Paul.

Goldtop '55–Rick Live Sherwood Lodge 1966

My first Gibson Les Paul that I bought, was a used 1955 Gibson Les Paul Goldtop # 5 9940, I found for sale at "The A" a used book store. A Goldtop with the gold tone – my first Les Paul '55 bought in 1965 for $65 they were only ten years old at that time but I still have that one that helped start my career. I took her with me everywhere I went. I had to sell so many instruments over the years but many left me for numerous trades and sorry to admit mostly for lack of money to live on. I'm making a list of the ones I wish I didn't sell or trade and it's pretty scary.

Thanks to one of my grandmother's, an avid postage stamp collector who also had a blue china plate collection, (Royal Delft Blue Plates with Birds) I started a collection of my own (not plates) in the 50s, first with coins and stamps, on to comics, baseball cards, next it was drums from 8 years old till my 7th Grade junior high school Band, where I was first chair on 2 instruments and Straight A's on both) and then one fine day I'd had enough with the band and the band director as I'd been around true professional musicians growing up, and this environment was not, I went in front of the class and blurted out for all to hear—"Mr Bueschel" "You're an incompetent drunken fool, who doesn't deserve to teach music, to me, or anyone else." Rick Nielsen 1962. I was immediately expelled and banned from the Rockford School System's Music Programs for life. My parents were pleased – 12 years old and banned from the band. Well, I guess I showed 'em.

The Nielsen Trust
25th September 2020 Rivets Stadium Loves Park, Illinois.
Rick's son Miles is playing 8 1948

Rick and Miles Nielsen

Daxx Nielsen

Rick Nielsen continued

My fascination with guitars started when I was 13 years old and over the past 50 years, I've bought, sold, traded, collected over 2000 instruments. I don't really have anywhere near that many anymore but like any other collector, I started with just one. My first Les Paul was the '55. It's no wonder for the last 70 years that so many of the top players, collectors and dreamers have held the original Gibson Les Paul's produced in Kalamazoo Michigan by some of the greatest instrument builders, those craftsmen that have to this day what many call "The Holy Grail" as an unparalleled value that back then with a price tag of $245.00 to today 1000 times that, and someway way more. The Goldtop was used on many Cheap Trick records and tours and this was my sound. My Sunbursts Flying Vs etc received a lot of attention but the Goldtop has always been cool and interwoven with my formative years.

It's no wonder for the last 70 years that so many of the top players, collectors and dreamers have held the original Gibson Les Paul's produced in Kalamazoo Michigan by some of the greatest instrument builders, those craftsmen that have to this day what many call "The Holy Grail" as an unparalleled value that back then with a price tag of $245.00 to today 1000 times that, and someway way more. The Goldtop was used on many Cheap Trick records and tours and this was my sound. My Sunburst's, Flying V's, Explorer's received a lot of attention but the Goldtop has always been cool and interwoven with my formative years.

You only have to think about the looks of that era and imagine a '50s dance band with matching suits, guitars and amps – These were heady and exciting years for young guitar slingers. Seeing stuff with Les and Mary on clips playing their Les Paul's was a huge influence. In the following years seeing others with a Goldtops, Danny Kirwan/Fleetwood Mac, Al Wilson/Canned Heat, Freddie King, Muddy Waters, Les Paul and Mary Ford, Clem Clemson/Alex Harvey, Hubert Sumlin, what a mighty feast of players.

courtesy of Rick – a rare sight of BB King with a Goldtop

Les was a great friend and appearing on stage at the N.Y. Iridium club created memories I will treasure forever.

I love this signed dollar bill

Photo credit: Mike Graham

Photo by Ralph Nielsen

Collecting and playing guitars has been a lifetime passion and many iconic guitars have passed through my hands during the hectic years of finding, buying, selling, trading and enjoying so many great and some not so great, but all unique works of art in my eyes, including over 200 Gibson Les Paul Models.

Here's me in 1969 in my parents' living room.

Still have these (left to right)
(#1) 51' Telecaster Paid $70
(#2) 59' Gibson Les Paul Standard Paid $215
(#3) 55' Gibson Les Paul Goldtop Paid $65
(#5) 57' Fender Sunburst Maple Neck Stratocaster - Paid $85
(#6) 57' Fender Sunburst Maple Neck Stratocaster Paid $90

Gone # 4-7-8
(# 4) 60' Gibson Les Paul Custom - Paid $165 Sold for $230
(# 7) 55' Fender Black Maple Neck Precision Bass Paid $130 Sold $225
(# 8) Mellotron Model MKII - Bought and brought from England Nov 1968

Times have changed

In 1968 I met and sold a Burst to Jeff Beck ($350), the 2nd Les Paul that he ever owned, I also owned # 0 1482 the rare 1960 left-handed Burst now in the hands of Paul McCartney. John Hammel, Paul McCartney's guitar tech quotes, "Paul's main stage guitar is a cherry sunburst 1960 Gibson Les Paul that we got from Rick Nielsen of Cheap Trick. Paul loves it. What's great about it is that it has the type of neck that they quit using when they brought out the SG-type Les Pauls. It has a great feel. For a backup electric, he also has a rare left-handed '57 Goldtop."

After my first meeting in Nashville with the new Gibson regime, they did some research and found my 55'Goldtop in one of their original ledger books (the ones they hadn't lost or thrown away) and there she is on the day she was born and shipped. They sent me this copy of the page.

Page 96, September 2, 1955- #5 9940

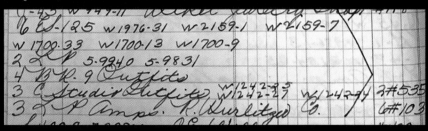

"Ain't It A Shame" 1955, Gold record award to Fats Domino. Back in the 50s when a single record a 45rpm sold 500,000 copies, the RIAA gave only 2 of these Gold records, one to the artist and one to the producer. Fats liked our version of "Ain't That A Shame" from "Cheap Trick Live At Budokan" so much that in 1979, his manager brought this Gold single award to our show in Salt Lake City as a gift. We drew straws and I've had it in my collection ever since. This is super rare, and such an honor from the man.

Rick

We thank Rick for sharing these early memories of his collecting passion and all he has done for the Burst Believers series 'a true star.'

Photo credit: Mike Slubowski

5 9957

Previously owned by **Ed King.**
It is now in the hands of Kris Blakely who
also purchased Ed's red 'Hot Rod' amplifier.

Photo credit: Ana Blakely Photography

510324

Courtesy of Sammy Ash

Richard Thompson

Few artists have been so successful with folk, electric folk and mainstream music. Richard Thompson has the wonderful talent to write songs which cover the full spectrum of human emotions. With his long career in the music world he continues to amaze us with poetic song writing, maintaining "I never really think about what songs mean, I just write them. Some of them reflect on what happened a few months ago or even a year ago. It's a process of surveying my life and where I was at." His guitar skills range from acoustic, often with a hard edge, to powerful rock with the guitar interweaving throughout the the songs delivering his very distinctive style so loved by his fans.

Richard belongs to the influential group of UK guitarists who adoped the Gibson Les Paul Goldtop during the 60's.

In 1969 manager Joe Boyd rented a cottage for Fairport Convention in Farley Chamberlayne to rehearse with new band members Dave Swarbrick and Dave Mattacks, I was invited to bring my camera and spend a weekend. It was a magical time.
Eric Hayes

Gibson Goldtop

The name Les Paul was familiar to me from a very young age. My dad, who played 'a bit' of guitar, had a couple of wonderful 78s of Les, so I was listening to the maestro inventing multitracking, double speed, slap echo etc, almost from before the time I could walk. WhenI started playing myself, I naturally used Les Paul guitar picks.
– If it was good enough for Les…

At age 18, I had turned professional, and my first 'proper' guitar was a big jazz Gibson 175D, wonderfully easy to play, but it fed back very annoyingly at rock and roll volume levels. In 1968, at a time before Customs and Excise caught on, an American came over to the UK with two Gibson Les Paul Goldtops, intent on a quick profit – it probably paid his airfare. I grabbed the one without the tailpiece, probably a '55. The holy grail at that time was the sunburst Les Paul with humbuckers, as used by Clapton, Peter Green, and every ranking British blues player, but that was beyond my budget, and you rarely saw on for sale – and I had never played one, so had no way to compare my PAFs with humbuckers. I loved the sound of the Goldtop, found the pickups mellow and responsive, and it suited the folk-rock style I was playing then with Fairport Convention. I used it on the second, third and fourth Fairport albums, right through 1968-69.

At some point, I wanted more bite in my sound. Some of my other guitar heroes were Fender players – Hank Marvin, James Burton, Jimmy Bryant, Robbie Robertson – and I got myself a Strat, and have been more of a Fender guy ever since. In those days, I couldn't afford to own a bunch of guitars, and had to sell the Goldtop to buy the Fender, alas! I sold it to John Martyn, who, within a week, had had it stolen.

I recently acquired a Gibson SG with 2 humbuckers, which I love, and which I've been using on a few things live and in the studio (yes, I can now afford to own two guitars). I wonder, from time to time, whatever happened to my old Goldtop. It had had a hard life before it reached me, judging by the wear on the neck and body, and I put many miles on it myself.
I hope it found a sympathetic, non-larcenous home.

Perhaps we'll meet again someday.

Richard Thompson

100 CLUB - Fairport Convention

It was Thursday, December 12, 1968. Fairport Convention was one of two bands playing that night at London's venerable 100 Club on Oxford Street. I had just come from the Intertel Studio in Wembly where the Rolling Stones Rock and Roll Circus was being filmed. When I later developed my roll of Tri-X I found that I had photos of Keith Richards and Richard Thompson on the same roll. Both are good company, you might say.

That these photos of Fairport in concert at the 100 Club still exist is nothing short of a miracle, in that I lost almost all my black & white negatives when I returned to Canada at the end of 1969. There were hundreds – no, thousands – of photographs of Hendrix, The Who, Led Zeppelin, Janis Joplin, Frank Zappa and many more – the culmination of a year-and-a-half's work in the music business. But my biggest disappointment was losing the work I had done of Richard Thompson, Sandy Denny and Fairport Convention in concert and in the recording studio. To find that I still had these few performance shots of the band was one of my happiest moments.

Eric Hayes

Author's comment
Thanks to Eric Hayes who was fortunate enough to capture these images from the Farley Chamberlayne rehearsals and the 100 Club concert. His recollections of these events provide us with a fascinating glimpse of these early days. We would also like to thank Richard Thompson and his management who assisted with the feature.

1955
510674

An early tune-o-matic bridge

Photo credit: Tony Nunzo

1955
513742

Thanks to Scot Arch
Photo credit: **Outside The Box Productionz**

513129 'Peggy'

The original owner was "Frikkie Wolfswinkle" a famous player in South Africa. A very late 1955 with stop tail with "bonnet knobs" The guitar was run over in its case back in the '60s breaking the neck at the heel and had two big wooden pegs put in the heel to repair it – it's still holding just fine today with no tuning problems whatsoever – a very resonant guitar. *JM*

Photo credit: Jim Mills

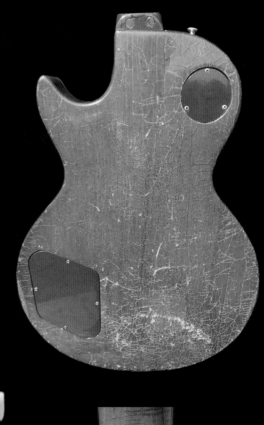

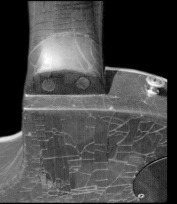

1955 Gibson Les Paul Humbucking Pickup Test Guitar

by Gil Hembree

Seth E. Lover (January 1, 1910, in Kalamazoo, Michigan – January 31, 1997) Seth died just before I found the guitar. In the late 1960s he moved California to work for Fender; that was because Gibson cancelled its amplifier business at that time.

Ted McCarty
August 21, 1999 Otsego, MI

Original guitar case

In the 1990s I paid for advertisements in many different Yellow Pages and local newspapers. I was advertising to buy vintage guitars from the original owner. In 1998 I received a call from a resident of Kalamazoo who saw my advertisement. Over the phone he described the guitar to me. It had early 1955 Gibson Les Paul Goldtop appointments but it had silver pickups. The guitar was from Kalamazoo, home of the 1950s factory on Parsons Street, so I thought anything might be possible. I owned a book, The Gibson (Japanese/English translation) which I referenced and looked at pictures of Seth Lover's first humbucker pickup built in 1955.

The owner traveled a lot so I was not able to see the guitar until November 21, 1998. I took The Gibson book with me. The first test was to see if the guitar had any hum. No hum; it was as quiet as could be. He gave me permission to gently pull the pickups up so I could see both front and back. The Gibson book had excellent photos of the front and back of Seth's first humbucking pickup. There was a picture of the back of the Seth Lover pickup which had very clear pencil script writing on the back of the pickup which identified aspects of the pickup. The two pickups on this guitar had the exact type of writing on the back of both pickups (it was done by the same person). I purchased the guitar at his asking price and my wife and I then returned to our home near Flint, MI. The owner told me his dad purchased the guitar in 1962 from a guy down the street. His dad did not play guitar but he enjoyed looking at the guitar hanging in the family living room.

Then I called Ted McCarty at the Bigsby factory in Kalamazoo. Ted said the guitar was the guitar used to test the new humbucking pickups. Ted identified the name Test Guitar. In early 1955 Ted had given Seth Lover the assignment of developing a quiet pickup that did not hum. Several of this type of pickup design already existed but Seth was told to develop a Gibson pickup that would sound something like a Gibson single-coil P-90, but without the hum. Seth's design was unique enough from pre-existing designs to the point that Seth's pickup would be an eligible design that could be covered by a Gibson patent. Seth went to Ted's office and slid the pickup across Ted's desk, announcing: "Here is your humbucker." Seth coined the term 'humbucking pickup.' Ted said: "put it on a guitar." Seth built two more pickups and the model makers put the pickups on a 1955 Gibson Les Paul Goldtop.

Gil Hembree and Ted McCarty with 1955 Gibson Les Paul Humbucking Test Guitar August 21, 1999 Otsego, MI

Wilbur Fuller worked closely with the model makes that created the Test Guitar. Note: he was cousin of Walter Fuller inventor Charlie Christian pickup.

1955 Gibson Les Paul Humbucking Pickup Test Guitar (continued)

by Gil Hembree

A completely built guitar was pulled out of the white wood inventory and taken to the model makers in the northeast section of the Parson's Street Factory basement. The new humbuckers were the same width and length as a P-90 but the humbuckers were deeper. The model makers hand routed new pickup cavities. The guitar was then taken to the 3rd floor spray booth and the guitar became a Goldtop. Then shielding paint and foil were added to both the potentiometer cavity and toggle switch cavity. Lover also reversed the two individual pickups so that they were out-of-phase with each other. Seth's idea was to have the humbuckers height adjustable at either side of the pickup. That meant a completely new pickup mounting design was needed. Seth did not plan to have individually adjustable pole pieces on this design. The model makers worked with Seth on the humbucker trim ring mounting design and it became the first design of its type to appear on a Gibson guitar (and the millions of humbucking equipped guitars to follow).

Finally, the 1955 Gibson Les Paul Humbucking Pickup Test guitar was ready for its test. Executives Ted McCarty, Julius Bellson, John Huis and Larry Allers were accompanied by players Rem Wall and Wilbur Marker in the Gibson conference room where the players played the guitar though a Gibson amplifier. The pickup readings were Bridge 7.2 and Neck 6.9. The sound was somewhat brighter than the PAF pickups build for production in early 1957. The guitar weighed 9.0 pounds. The guitar passed the test and absolutely no hum was emitted by the guitar and amp. Rollo Werner was called in to prepare a bill of material and understand the parts needed for the all new humbucker pickup. Eventually, the 1955 Gibson Les Paul Humbucking Pickup Test Guitar was retired to a closet in Julius Bellson's office.

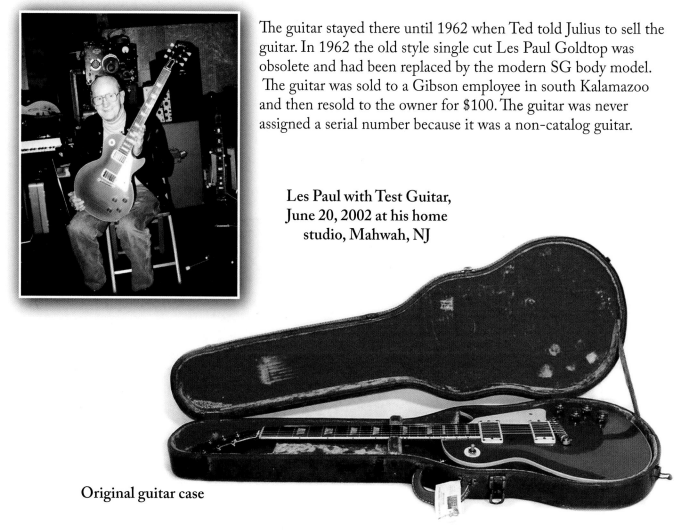

The guitar stayed there until 1962 when Ted told Julius to sell the guitar. In 1962 the old style single cut Les Paul Goldtop was obsolete and had been replaced by the modern SG body model. The guitar was sold to a Gibson employee in south Kalamazoo and then resold to the owner for $100. The guitar was never assigned a serial number because it was a non-catalog guitar.

**Les Paul with Test Guitar,
June 20, 2002 at his home
studio, Mahwah, NJ**

Original guitar case

New mounting ring used with the Test Guitar humbucking pickups

Bridge pickup underside and routing

Neck pickup with cover removed

Joyce Shelven (hired 1952) she was in the white wood hand sanding department

Harriet Johnston (hired 1944) and was the 2nd floor stock room clerk

Mary Lou Hoogenboom (hired 1953)and was in the white wood hand sanding department

Clara Van Noorloos (hired in 1943) and worked in stringroom

Thanks to Gil for documenting these historical photographs of these employees at the time of the Test Guitar Kalamazoo MI September 30, 2002.

Photo credit: Viktor Nemeth

6 4747

Thanks to Gary Dick

GARY'S
CLASSIC
GUITARS
LLC

1956 Les Paul Standard ALL GOLD. Stunningly clean and all-original. Besides having an ALL GOLD finish, this very rare example has a Stop Tailpiece, sans the Tune-o-matic bridge of this period. This is the 2nd All Gold, Stop Tailpiece 1956 Standard that I have personally seen. I surmise the guitars were built in 1955, drilled for the Stop Tailpiece, prior to the new Tune-o-maticbridge update, but for some reason, were finished and shipped the following year. The other example is stamped as a "2nd."

Photos and Feature by Albert Molinaro

610666

612340

Thanks to Matt King
Photo credit: Penelope King

613345

Photo credit: Ana Blakely Photography

615279

A clean example of a great playing
and sounding '56 Goldtop with the
desirable tune-o-matic bridge
and tail piece.

Photo credit: Mike Slubowski

Danny Kirwan

Danny Kirwan's biggest success came with playing guitar with Fleetwood Mac from 1968 to 1972 . He also released three solo albums after leaving the band. Danny used a circa 1956 Goldtop with Fleetwood Mac in his early years and eventually switched over to a burst. His playing style complimented Peter Green very well. Together these two guitarists laid down some of the best English blues tracks ever recorded. They were dynamic as a team.

One of Danny's highlight songs was "Jigsaw Puzzle Blues." This era of Fleetwood Mac is still held in high regards with musicians and blues rock lovers.

7 0232

This early 1957 Goldtop has all the features a Les Paul should usually have in this era. Light back mahogany body with brown backplates, bonnet knobs and of course a tune-o-matic bridge. By mid year this model will have the new humbucking pickups which will replace the P 90's.

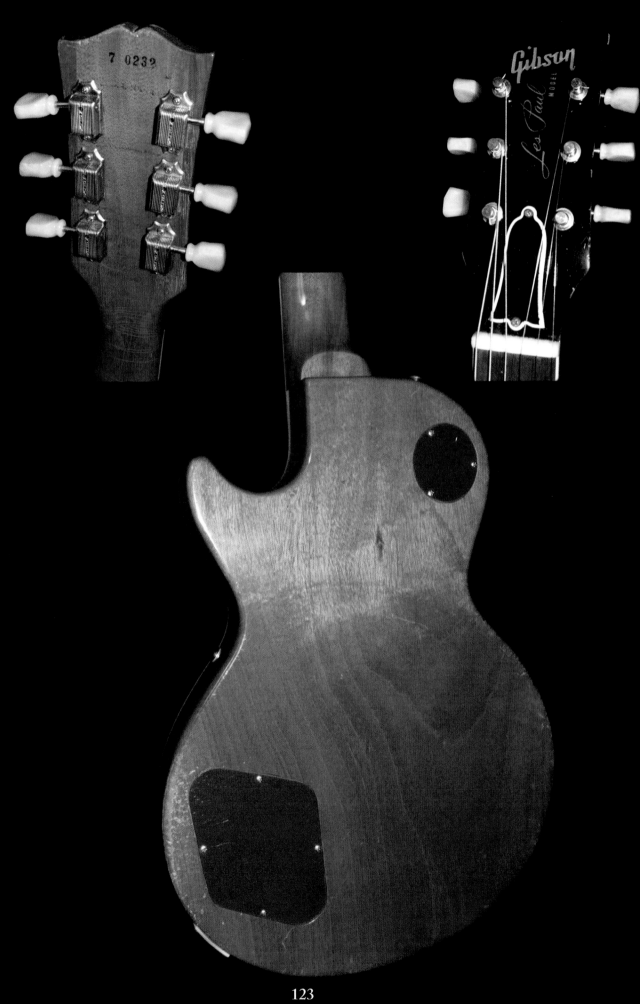

7 1879

Courtesy of Miraldo Vidal

1957 the first appearance of Humbuckers

Thanks to Jim Mills for sharing this super rare document of Gibson history. It is totally original, dated April 26th, 1957. A letter from Gibson to their Dealers and in the next to the last paragraph mentioning one of the first references to the PAF Humbucker – they call it "Humbuck! This sales list/update for Gibson Dealers was typed for none other than Gibson Sales Manager, the infamous Mr Clarence Havenga. It begs the question. 'Were Goldtop Les Paul's as well as 175's sporting PAF's by April of 1957 as well'. We know they made the change in '57 but have never heard anyone definitively say exactly when the change from P-90's to the PAF's appeared on the LP.

Don't be alarmed --
Gibson prices have not gone up!

It's just that so many new items have been added to the line during the past few months that we've had to print a new price list showing the present complete line. Let us point out some of the new instruments that are helping to make Gibson more valuable to you than ever...

Three new 3/4-size guitars for young students or folks with small hands...the Les Paul Jr. 3/4, ES-125 3/4 Thin and the ES-140 3/4 Thin.

In standard-size thin guitars, new models include the ES-225 TN natural finish with one pickup, ES-225 TD in regular or natural finish with two pickups and toggle switch, and the ES-125T.

A completely different Mandolin with amazing tone and volume - Style A-5 Florentine design with round sound hole.

In steel guitars, a new Console, Model C-530, replaces the Consolette; we have a new Triple Neck, CG-523, which has the same styling as the new Console Grande, with 4-8-4 pickups; and there is the new Multiharp Triple Neck steel with six pedals on the middle neck.

A new low-priced Classic guitar will be available soon, Model C-1, at $89.50...a tremendous value in appearance and tone.

J-45 and J-50 jumbo guitars are now available with adjustable bridges at no extra charge. Several hundred have been in use for months with complete satisfaction.

Models ES-175-D and ES-175-DN are now available with the sensational new Humbuck pickups which offer so much more sustaining power and clarity of tone while greatly reducing hum and extraneous noises from electrical disturbances such as neon lights, etc.

Our delivery schedule is improving, thanks to your help in anticipating your future needs. With your continued cooperation, we shall hope to do even better. Use the enclosed prepaid form to bring your Gibson display up to full sales strength.

Sincerely yours,

CHICAGO MUSICAL INSTRUMENT CO.

Clarence Havenga
Sales Manager - Gibson Division

CH/mwb
enclosures

CHICAGO MUSICAL INSTRUMENT CO., • EXCLUSIVE DISTRIBUTORS

127

7 2342
The Striker

This 1957 Les Paul kicks off our introduction of the humbucking pickup fitted on a solid body guitar. The Les Paul Custom was also fitted with the new pickups the same year. Many of the early Goldtops in the 7 2000 serial number range had black parts including the pickup rings, pickguard, rhythm/treble poker chip and the jack plate. Also noteworthy is that many of these early Goldtops had dark mahogany colored backs and necks and no "Patent Applied For" stickers attached to the bottom of the base of the pickup.

Photo credit: Viktor Nemeth

Brian Ray

7 2399

Thanks to Brian for his assistance with th
feature and Eleanor Jane for the photogr
which is featured on Guitar.com"

130

The year was 1973 and I was a senior in high school when I invited my high school bandmates over to my sister's house in Malibu one day to pick up my new vintage Gibson Les Paul. My friends and I crowded around the old brown Lifton case as I popped it open, and saw this beautiful, well loved 1957 Goldtop Les Paul with Humbuckings. My sister's boyfriend at the time sold it to me for the princely sum of $850, which of course at that time was a lot of money. He bought the guitar at We Buy Guitars in New York City for $550, and I was a little bit piqued at him for taking an outrageous profit of $300! That Guitar became my best friend through which I could express feelings that I couldn't find the words for as a young kid growing up. Soon afterwards, I got an audition with Etta James, after which she invited me to play a show the next night in Long Beach, which led to 30 years of deep friendship, respect and collaboration, both as her guitarist, musical director, and later as producer and co-writer. I played every show except one with Etta James on that same Les Paul.

I restored the guitar in 1987 with a guy name Steve Soest, reuniting the guitar with every screw and wire that would've been on the guitar originally. The guitar is my number one, always has, and always will be.

It's a remarkable instrument and it's as close to me as a sibling.
Bryan Ray

Tokyo Dome 2013

131

Photo credit: Daimir Slabolovic

Thanks to Gary Dick

7 2916

This road warrior has a push/pull pot installed on the bridge pickup, copper shield tape on the back of control plate cover and had a headstock repair. With several refrets, this iconic guitar is a great example of a working instrument.

Snowy White

Snowy White bought the Goldtop in 1969 from the original owner in Sweden. It was a trade for a '50s Stratocaster plus £120. It remained his principal guitar throughout his career until 2015 when sold to a Burst Believer contributor.

"Let's get one thing straight, I know nothing about guitars. I haven't a clue about pick-ups or wiring or why they work. Not actually interested. All I wanted to do was play tasteful blues phrases over simple chords. That's the only reason I learned to play, I wanted to know what it FELT like. And I soon discovered that to get the sound I wanted I needed a Les Paul. That's when my old Goldtop entered my life.

What a great guitar it turned out to be. I got lucky. It was with me for 45 years, and in the early days, I carried it everywhere with me, didn't like to leave it in dressing rooms or hotels, so it's been to a lot of interesting places, and a lot of decent restaurants. It has travelled the world with me many times. Roasted in North Africa, frozen in Finland. I rescued it from our burning car after a crash near Nashville, and once I left it in my unlocked car on a London street all night with the door slightly open and it was still there in the morning. One foggy early morning I was catching a flight to Belgium and I backed over it as I reversed sleepily out of my garage. Forgot to put it in the car. The case was buried in the gravel but my old trusty Les Paul was perfectly fine.

We have had many adventures together. If it could talk it could get me into a lot of trouble. After all these years of, well, I have to be honest here, mistreatment, it still always stays perfectly in tune and sings sweetly on every fret. I liked the memories that coated its scratched and faded paintwork, so whenever a new guitar tech came along, my first instruction was, whatever you do, DON'T clean it. But all good things come to an end, and we have finally parted company. It was time to move on, clear the decks. I wish I hadn't sold it but I'm glad I did. No, that doesn't make sense to me either."

Snowy White

Thanks to Snowy White and Matt Swanson for organising this feature

Charlie Starr

BLACKBERRY SMOKE

What would the world be like if Les Paul, Ted McCarty and Gibson hadn't supplied us with their fabulous creation, the Les Paul Model? I shudder to think of it. How could they have known what our ears would be yearning to hear all these decades later? You can keep your sliced bread.
I'll take a Les Paul.

7 3145

This particular guitar has quite a story, as I understand it. Apparently, it's a 1953 Les Paul model that made its way back to Kalamazoo in 1957 for some updates and/or maybe repair. It appears to have been given a black finish, a Bigsby tailpiece, a bumblebee cap to accompany a grey tiger and a '57 serial number. At some point, it seems that someone tried a 7-string conversion on this thing, but maybe thought better of it and removed all that nonsense. More recently, it appears to have received a headstock repair and some finish work there, so it obviously sounds better, right? Anyhow, it's obviously lived through some things and come out the other side playing, looking and sounding great.

Gotta love 'em

Charlie

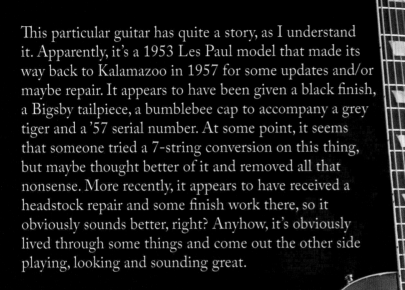

Duane Allman

After Duane Allman died in 1971, his famous 1957 Les Paul Goldtop would change hands but would finally end up with Scot LaMar. Scot rescued this piece of rock history and restored it to its original condition. The original style gold finish restoration was done by Tom Murphy. The guitar has been loaned out for live gigs to Warren Haynes, Derek Trucks, Vince Gill and a few others. Now residing at The Big House Museum in Macon, Georgia. This iconic Les Paul Goldtop sold at an auction for 1.25 million dollars. Many refer to this Les Paul as the 'Layla' Goldtop.

Thanks to Richard Brent 'The Big House' for this feature.

7 3312 'Layla' – Duane Allman

Photo credit: Charlie Daughtry

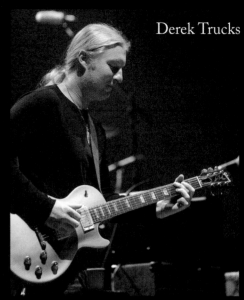

Derek Trucks

Vince Gill and Lee Roy Parnell

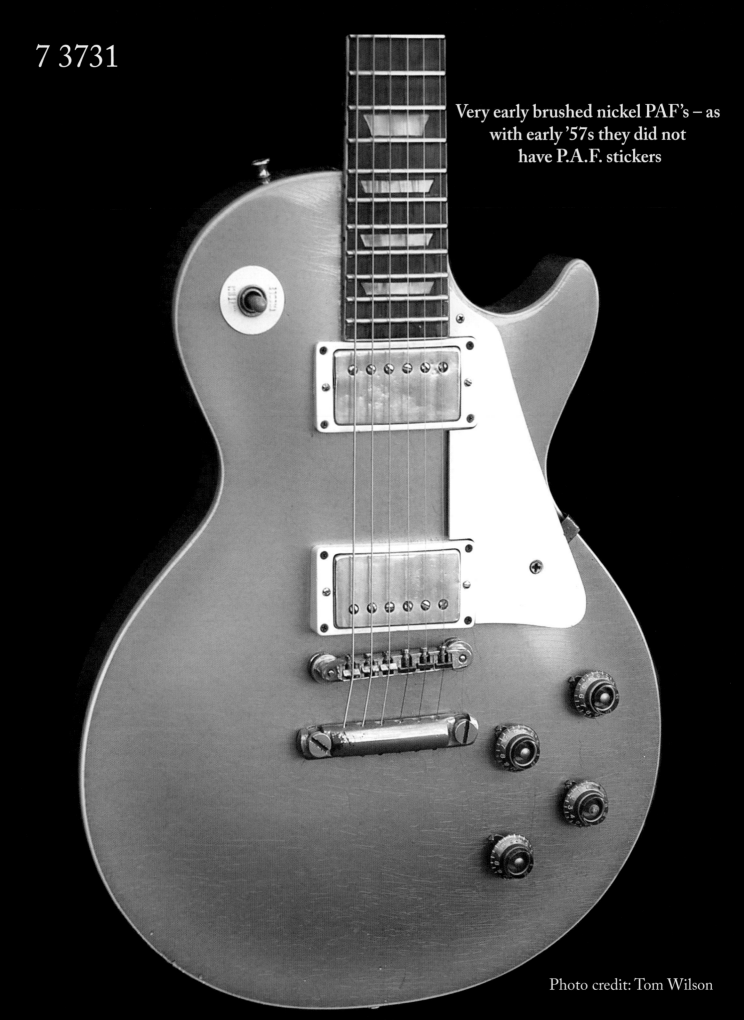

7 3731

Very early brushed nickel PAF's – as
with early '57s they did not
have P.A.F. stickers

A super clean example

7 3969

showing the worn gold paint on the lower
horn from the owner's style of picking

Courtesy of Damir Slabolovic

7 4401 'Gloria'

The guitar left the factory with a stop tail, a Bigsby was fitted in 1963 and later removed. A unique feature is the factory "stinger" on the back of the headstock.

Photo credit: Neil Salamack

Thanks to Dave Rogers
and Tim Mullally

7.6181

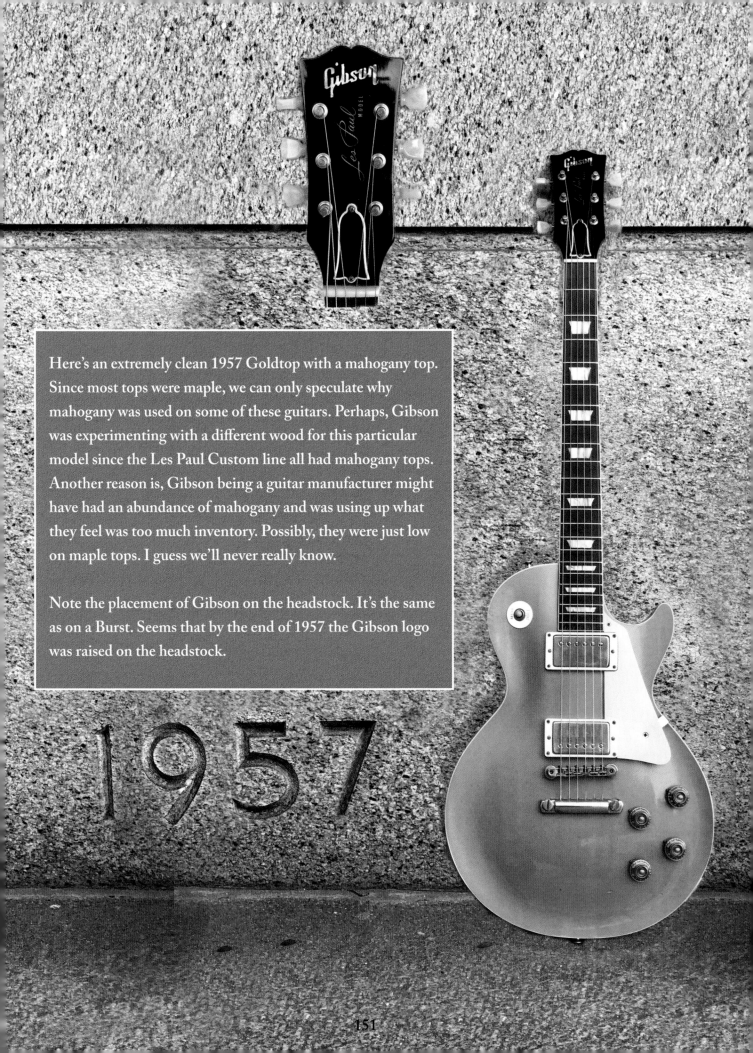

Here's an extremely clean 1957 Goldtop with a mahogany top. Since most tops were maple, we can only speculate why mahogany was used on some of these guitars. Perhaps, Gibson was experimenting with a different wood for this particular model since the Les Paul Custom line all had mahogany tops. Another reason is, Gibson being a guitar manufacturer might have had an abundance of mahogany and was using up what they feel was too much inventory. Possibly, they were just low on maple tops. I guess we'll never really know.

Note the placement of Gibson on the headstock. It's the same as on a Burst. Seems that by the end of 1957 the Gibson logo was raised on the headstock.

7 7322

Photo credit: Mike Slubowski

152

7 7499

Photo credit: Bruce Sandler
Guitar Exchange

153

Solid mahogany, no maple cap.
weighing a modest 8lb 12oz.

Geoff Whitehorn

I bought the guitar from Guitar Village (Top Gear's other branch) in Shaftesbury Avenue for £350 in August 1972. It was my 21st birthday present to myself. I replaced the Kluson Tuners with Grovers and had the guitar re-fretted by Sam Li, who was THE guy in the West End at the time. The original frets were tiny so they had to go. Used on all the IF and Crawler stuff and on a lot of my session work. I haven't gigged it much since the late '70s.

Geoff

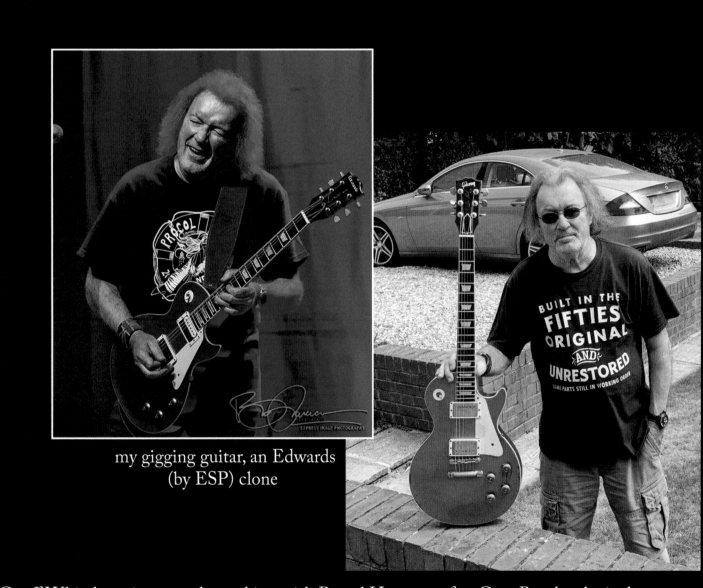

my gigging guitar, an Edwards
(by ESP) clone

Geoff Whitehorn is currently working with Procol Harum – after Gary Brooker, he is the longest serving member (1991). His career started in 1973 with the progressive jazz rock band 'if', later renamed IF. He would replace Paul Kossoff in Crawler from 1976 to 1979 transforming from jazz rock to mainstream rock. Working with artists such as Bad Company, Elkie Brooks, The Who, Roger Waters, Manfred Mann's Earth Band, Paul McCartney, Billy Ocean and Paul Rodgers he is in great demand for session and live performance work.

Joe Bonamassa

Joe Bonamassa has a passion for vintage instruments and amps. Goldtops were an early favourite, especially the '57 with the black plastic pickups and guard. Gibson manufactured a very successful run of these guitars under the Epiphone brand.

Photo credit: Charlie Daughtry

7 6982

Joe recently acquired this stunningly clean '57

Photo credit: Rick Gould

Steve Hackett 1957

I have a Goldtop 1957 Les Paul guitar with humbucker pickups. This guitar still makes a wonderful noise. It was the sound of Eric Clapton's Les Paul on John Mayall's Blues Breakers album that left me breathless at that time. Although that album was recorded in 1966, it still features heavily in the heaven of rock guitarists whom I've worked with, including Brian May and Steve Howe. The combination of the Gibson Les Paul plus a heavily cranked Marshall amp was a kind of magical musical mountain top that we were all aiming to reach.
I still use my 1957 Les Paul mainly for recording as it's too precious to risk on the road. It's heard to best effect on the finale of my track 'Those Golden Wings' from my latest album At The Edge Of Light.

Steve Hackett

Steve Hackett is renowned as an immensely talented and innovative rock musician. He was lead guitarist with Genesis as part of their classic line up with Gabriel, Collins, Banks and Rutherford, that produced acclaimed albums such as 'Selling England by the Pound' (a favourite of John Lennon). With Steve's extraordinary versatility in both his electric guitar playing and his composing, he involves influences from many genres, including Jazz, World Music and Blues.

With Genesis, Steve's guitar playing produced some of the most memorable moments, from the sensitivity of his acoustic sound on 'Horizons and Blood on the Rooftops' to the dramatic rock guitar solos of 'Firth'.

He embarked on his solo career and developed his exceptional range, pushing musical boundaries into exiting areas, inventing new sounds and also techniques such as 'tapping'. His solo career went from strength to strength and the mid-eighties not only saw the hit single 'Cell 151', but also the Steve Hackett and Steve Howe super group GTR, highly successful in America.

After GTR Steve worked further with many renowned musicians such as Paul Carrick, Bonny Tyler, John Wetton and Brian May, who has credited Steve as an early influence. Steve went on to produce his hit album 'Genesis Revisited'. He went even further back to his roots with 'Blues with a Feeling', whilst continuing to challenge his own horizons with an amazing eclectic mix of sounds, genres and a sense of the exotic that incites his many followers to this day.

Recent albums possessed a high level of sophistication, along with ever-present powerful dynamic, for the dramatic and atmospheric darkness of 'Darktown and Wild Orchids' to the colourful voyage through time and space of 'To Watch the Storms'.

Thanks to Steve and Sharon Chevin (The Publicity Connection) for this feature
also the biography extracted from www.stevehackett.com

Dickey Betts

Dickey Betts is recognized as one of rock's greatest guitarists. He's best known for his collaboration with Duane Allman in the Allman Brothers Band. The two of them played melodic twin harmony guitar parts which became a staple in their songs. Dickey wrote the band's only hit single "Ramblin Man" a country rock song with dual harmony lead guitar phrases. Dickeys main guitar was a 1957 PAF Goldtop which he later had it refinished red in place of the worn original gold finish. Betts was inducted into the Rock 'n Roll Hall Of Fame in 1995.

Photo credit: Charlie Daughtry

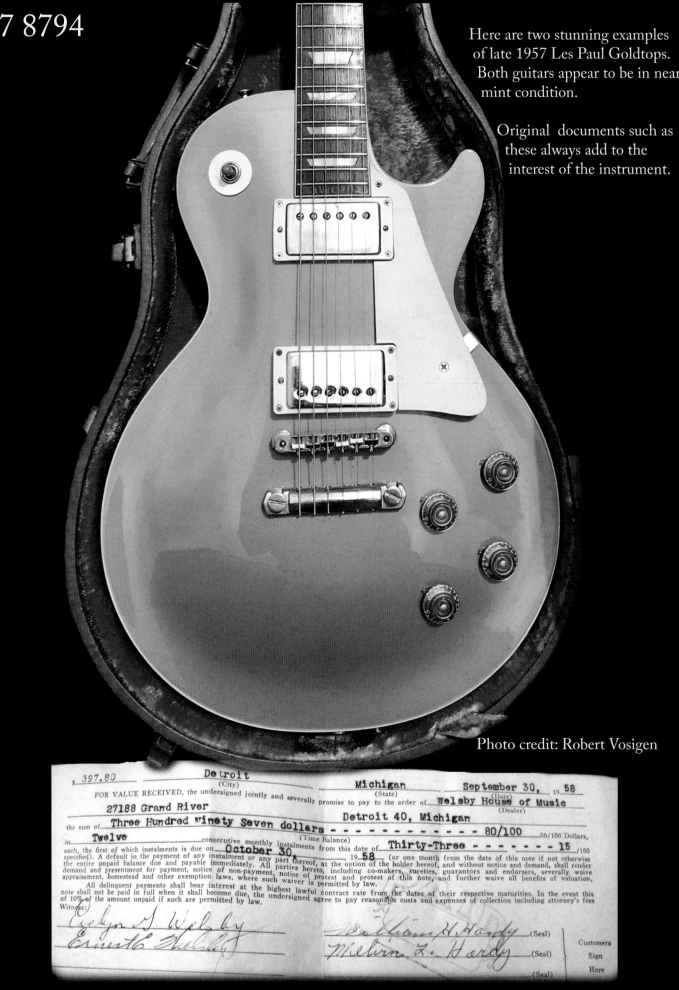

Here are two stunning examples
of late 1957 Les Paul Goldtops.
Both guitars appear to be in near
mint condition.

Original documents such as
these always add to the
interest of the instrument.

Photo credit: Robert Vosigen

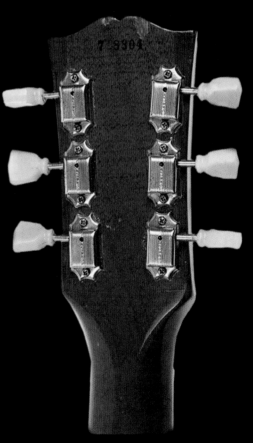

Photo credit: Tom Allen

8 1009

Clem Clempson
(part one)

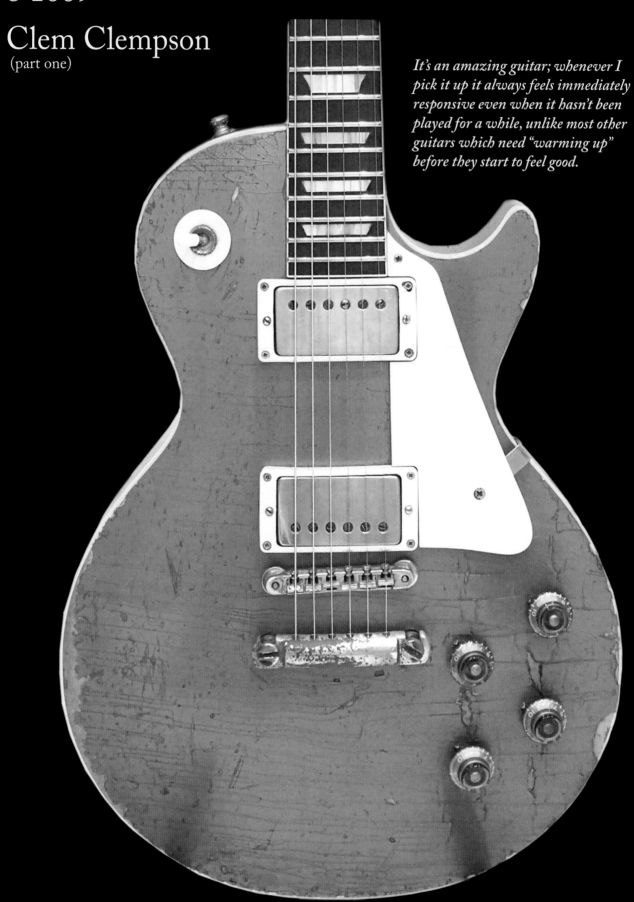

It's an amazing guitar; whenever I pick it up it always feels immediately responsive even when it hasn't been played for a while, unlike most other guitars which need "warming up" before they start to feel good.

Playing with Colosseum, Humble Pie, Cozy Powell and Jack Bruce, Clem has appeared with many top bands, collaborated with great musicians and played on countless recording sessions. His guitar of choice,

the Gibson Les Paul Goldtop.

However here's a little background on my acquisition of the Goldtop: a friend of mine, Tony Crosby, a student from Nottingham, bought it from Ringway Music in Birmingham during a visit to stay with me and Terry Poole. I was rather sick that I'd missed the chance to buy it myself because I visited Ringway regularly and had already bought a couple of guitars from them, and it was my dream at the time to get my hands on a Les Paul! However a few weeks later Tony made me an offer; he had no amplifier and no money left after paying £300 for the Goldtop. He said he would be prepared to part with the Goldtop in exchange for an SG Standard and a Marshall head. I was playing a 335 at the time, so I immediately travelled down from Tamworth to London and exchanged my 335 for an SG, went directly from there to Nottingham and finally my dream came true when I took possession of the Goldtop that has been with me ever since!

Clem

Steve Marriott, Dave "Clem" Clempson and Greg Ridley of Humble Pie perform on stage in Bilzen, Belgium, Aug. 17, 1974. (Photo by Gijsbert Hanekroot). Courtesy Alamy

Clem Clempson (part 2)

Clem only began to develop a serious interest in music upon being taken to see "Rock Around The Clock" on its UK release in the late 50s, at which point a fascination with the electric guitar began to take hold. As with so many young lads at the time this interest was further stoked at the beginning of the 60s by the records and TV appearances of The Shadows, featuring the first British guitar hero, Hank Marvin. Clem by 1963 managed to save the £5 needed for the purchase of his first guitar, fitting it with a £2 electric pick-up. A band the Vipers were formed at Atherstone Grammar School and Clem's career as a guitarist was off the ground. However, things were about to be shaken up considerably by the release in 1966 of the classic "Bluesbreakers with Eric Clapton" LP. Eric's ferocious soloing, particularly on the slow blues "Have You Heard", was a revelation. Although this wasn't Clem's first exposure to the blues, having heard tracks by Muddy Waters, Howlin Wolf, John Lee Hooker and more, the power of Eric's approach to playing this music instantly touched a nerve and set Clem off on a mission to play the blues!

When this legendary album was followed very quickly by the first albums from Cream and Jimi Hendrix., which took the blues generation a step further, Clem knew that playing chart hits in working men's clubs couldn't satisfy his musical inclinations. So, when he was approached by top local band "The Pinch" he had no hesitation in joining – they were like-minded musically, and were getting gigs in colleges and other larger venues, where there was an audience for the music Clem was so excited about, and where the band wasn't constantly being warned to keep the volume down! The band consisted of Clem, drummer John Hinch, and bassist David Mason, who was very soon replaced by Terry Poole, whereupon the first incarnation of what was to become Bakerloo was born. The band was by now performing frequently around the Birmingham area, and was approached by local manager and trumpet player Jim Simpson, who was looking after the successful Locomotive. Jim was appointed manager of the band, and it was decided that a change of name was needed to reflect the music the band was intent on playing, and on returning from a trip to London Jim suggested Bakerloo Blues Line. Due to a shortage of Blues venues around Birmingham at that time the band and Jim collaborated in 1968 on opening a club, Henry's Blues House, in a room above The Crown public house. BBL performed there most Tuesday evenings at that time, and as word spread more and more like-minded young musicians began to turn up for a blues jam, and the audience had the chance to see the likes of John Bonham, Robert Plant, Cozy Powell, Jethro Tull, Climax Blues Band and the members of Black Sabbath, along with many other local musicians, all at an early stage on their respective musical journeys. The musicians all shared a commitment to good music and a determination to make a career of it – some of them did rather well!!!

A major milestone in Clem's career began with the visit to Henry's by impresario Tony Hall to hear Bakerloo Blues Line perform, culminating in a record deal with EMI which would make the band's debut album one of the first releases on the new "underground" Harvest label. It was decided at this time to shorten the name to simply "Bakerloo." Subsequently the band was booked into Trident studios in London to record "Bakerloo", which was basically just a recording of the band's live set. It was also the first production by Gus Dudgeon, who had engineered The Bluesbreakers Album and went on to achieve massive success as producer for Elton John amongst others.

At the same time, a club in Erdington was emerging as one of the country's top music venues – it was called Mothers and Bakerloo soon found themselves booked to play there on a regular basis. It was here that John Peel heard the band and an invitation was immediately issued to appear on John's hugely influential "Top Gear" show. The show was broadcast on October 20th 1968, and a huge demand was immediately created for the band to perform at the many blues clubs that were now springing up all over the UK, as well as the long-established music meccas such as London's Marquee Club. Performing there was the realisation of a dream for Clem, and, in fact the band was offered one of the venue's legendary and coveted residencies. Another important source of work for the up and coming bands of the time was the college circuit, and the next milestone in Clem's career happened on May 8th, 1969, when Bakerloo was booked to play at Cambridge University as support to a thrilling new band called Colosseum, who had made a huge impression on Clem when he went to hear them at Mothers. Coincidentally Bakerloo was to split soon after this gig. Clem and Cozy Powell had meanwhile become great mates and often spoke of forming a band together, so after Dave Pegg had been recruited on bass rehearsals began. The trio fulfilled an outstanding Bakerloo engagement at Sheffield University, and on the evidence of that the band seemed to have a bright future – but sadly it was to be the only gig the band would ever play. A few days later a message was delivered, via Mothers boss Phil Myatt, that Jon Hiseman had been impressed with what he'd heard at Cambridge and would like to meet up with Clem to discuss the prospect of his replacing James Litherland as guitarist in Colosseum.

Clem set about learning all the tracks on Colosseum's "Those About To Die" LP, and was soon on the train to London for a meeting in the band's rehearsal facility in Elephant and Castle. After meeting the band members it was time for Clem to plug in his 1958 Les Paul Goldtop, and after an exhilarating run-through of the title track from "Those About" Clem was instantly offered the job as guitarist and lead vocalist with one of the country's most exciting and innovative bands!

Cozy and Dave Pegg were understandably disappointed about this turn of events, but they'd both very soon be offered gigs with Jeff Beck and Fairport Convention respectively, so it all ended very well for all, and the three remained the best of friends for many years.

'Clem' Clempson has moved...

...to Laney

There were many memorable times ahead, starting with Clem's first ever flight for one of his first Colosseum gigs, in Prague, which was still under Russian occupation. The band was building a formidable reputation at gigs and festivals all over Europe, including the legendary Bath festival on Saturday, June 7th 1970, and the 1970 Fehmarn festival in Germany, an occasion which marked Jimi Hendrix's last gig and Clem's 21st birthday.

Chris Farlowe and Mark Clarke completed the "classic" Colosseum line-up for the recording of the Daughter of Time album, followed by Colosseum Live, and with the exception of Dick Heckstall-Smith, who sadly succumbed to a long illness in 2004 and was replaced by Barbara Thompson, this line-up continues to tour and record – albeit after a brief interruption of 22 years, which began with Clem's decision in 1972 to accept an invitation from Steve Marriott to join Humble Pie.

Clem Clempson (part 3)

After just a handful of gigs the new Pie line-up bega work in Olympic Studios on the Smokin' album. One of Clem's favourite records in recent years had been Crosby, Stills, Nash and Young's Deja Vu, so the sudden and unexpected appearance of Stephen Stills in the studio one evening was an unforgettable moment, and his subsequent contribution of a brilliant vocal line (Do you get the message?) for Hot 'n' Nasty helped the track become a hit single and one of the Pie's most popular tracks to this day. Clem was also delighted to have the chance to sing a duet on the album with a gentleman who had become something of a mentor when, in the early days of Bakerloo, the pair jammed on stage at "Les Cousins" – the great Alexis Korner.

Much fun on the road ensued as the band toured the USA endlessly, selling out the biggest venues in the country including the Philadelphia Spectrum, Detroit's Cobo Hall and Madison Square Gardens as well as such legendary venues as San Francisco's Winterland, the Warehouse in New Orleans and the Academy of Music in New York. There were also tours in the UK, Europe and, memorably, Japan.

Somehow the band also managed to record a further three albums – Eat It, Thunderbox, and Street Rats – before the stress of the hectic schedule, combined with serious concerns about the policies of the band's management, finally took its toll and the band split.

After the break-up of Humble Pie came another doomed attempt to join up with Cozy Powell, tentatively called Strange Brew and also including Greg Ridley. This time the plan was sabotaged by Clem breaking his left wrist whilst playing football – the very cheerful nurse while putting the wrist in plaster mentioned that it was possible Clem would permanently lose the grip in his left hand – a depressing prospect for an ambitious guitarist, although the nurse was quick to point out that things weren't so bad, as Clem was right-handed and so would have no problem with writing! Fortunately, everything turned out ok with the wrist, but during the recovery period Cozy was offered the gig with Ritchie Blackmore's Rainbow, so once again plans for a collaboration were shelved.

Another of the landmarks of Clem's career came at this time when Cozy Powell asked him to play on a couple of tracks for his first solo album, Over The Top. The tracks were "The Loner", a beautiful ballad, and "Sweet Poison" both written by Max Middleton. Playing bass on the album was one of Clem's heroes, Jack Bruce and Clem was thrilled to have the chance to work with him, especially when an appearance on the BBC's legendary live music show The Old Grey Whistle Test was lined up to promote Cozy's album. The band sounded great, performing "Killer" and "The Loner." On keyboards was Don Airey who also started his professional career with Colosseum.

Soon after the collaboration on Cozy's album, Jack showed up at Clem's home and said he was planning a new band, with Billy Cobham on drums and David Sancious on keyboards – would Clem be interested in playing guitar? This was a wonderful opportunity for a return to the kind of music Clem had enjoyed playing with Colosseum, who had included several Jack Bruce compositions in their repertoire.

David and Billy were sensational musicians, so it was an extremely exciting prospect, which was to begin with rehearsals in New York in early 1980. An album, "I've Always Wanted To Do This", was recorded at the House of Music in New Jersey, followed by tours of the US and Europe. It was a lot of fun, and highly acclaimed by critics and fans, but in the end not as commercially successful as had been hoped, and the band split without making any further recordings.

Clem and David Sancious had become close friends during their time with Jack, and when Clem was approached by Jon Anderson to work on a new album (Clem had already played on some tracks for Jon's previous LP "Song of Seven") he recommended David for the keyboards role. An album, "Animation" was recorded at Jon's studio in London and a major US tour was arranged to coincide with the release of the album in the summer of 1982. Clem and Jack continued to work together throughout the 80s, with several different drummers and usually with their mutual friend Ronnie Leahy on keyboards. *(Author's note: In 1983 I had the great pleasure seeing this lineup in a small night club and was blown away with sheer power of the group. DP)*

A very special highlight of the collaboration with Jack was the 1993 Cologne concert to mark Jack's 50th birthday, which featured various combinations of many of Jack's former colleagues including Ginger Baker, Dick Heckstall-Smith, Simon. Meanwhile, the 1980s and 90s also saw Clem in great demand as a session guitarist, working on recordings by Roger Daltrey, Tanita Tikaram, Mike and the Mechanics, Rod Argent, Paul McCartney, Roger Waters, Aaron Neville, Maxi Priest, Chris Farlowe, Bob Dylan (the disastrous film "Hearts of Fire"), Joshua Kadison, Andrew Lloyd Webber, Kiri Te Kanawa and many others, plus numerous film soundtracks, including Notting Hill, Lawn Dogs, Sweet Home Alabama, White Palace, Buddy's Song, Dead Dog Blues, Gangster No. 1 and Message in a Bottle. Phillips, Gary Husband and Gary Moore. A CD of the concert, "Cities of the Heart" was released. During this period Clem also stepped up his composition work, writing music for TV and films – much of which is still being used in productions all over the world, and has been featured in such programmes as The Simpsons, Baywatch, Sex and the City, Beavis and Butthead and The Good Sex Guide! Clem's proudest achievement in the session world came in 2005 when he worked as guitarist and unofficial musical director with one of his biggest influences, and one of the blues genre's most important musicians, BB King, on tracks for an album commemorating BB's 80th birthday, "BB King and Friends 80". Many top names contributed to the record, and the tracks Clem played on featured BB in vocal duets with Roger Daltrey and Van Morrison, as a result of which Clem received a phone call from Van's management inquiring whether the post of musical director for Van Morrison would be of interest to Clem!

Colosseum recorded a new CD "Time On Our Side" in spring 2014 and subsequently played their final tour of Europe, bringing down the final curtain on the legendary band at London's Shepherds Bush Empire on February 28th, 2015. In 2017 The band JCM was formed and performed until the tragic death in 2018 of Clem's great friend John Hiseman.
Today Clem continues working with 'the Clem Clemptson Band – a great Les Paul player with an amazing career.

Thanks to Clem and his permission to use his biography extracted from www.clemclempson.com

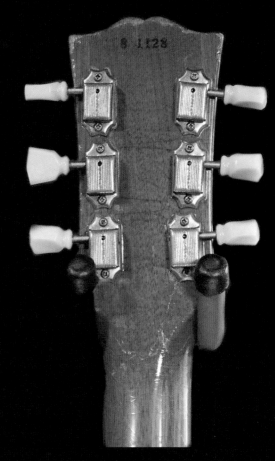

Vince Gill is more often seen playing
Fender guitars but he is equally at home
with his Burst as seen in Burst Believers V
or with this '58 Goldtop.

Once again we thank him for his support
and providing access to his guitar collection.

Thanks to our good freind Jim Mills for assisting with this feature.

8 1131

Thanks to Dave Rogers
and Tim Mullally

8 1160

Thanks to Scot Arch
Photo credit: **Outside The Box Productionz**

8 1689 'Sweet Cherry'

We are proud and very excited to have this extremely rare 1958 Special order cherry red Les Paul Model in the book. The guitar is in near mint condition and retains all of its original color. We want to thank **Joe Menza** for sharing this rare beauty with us.

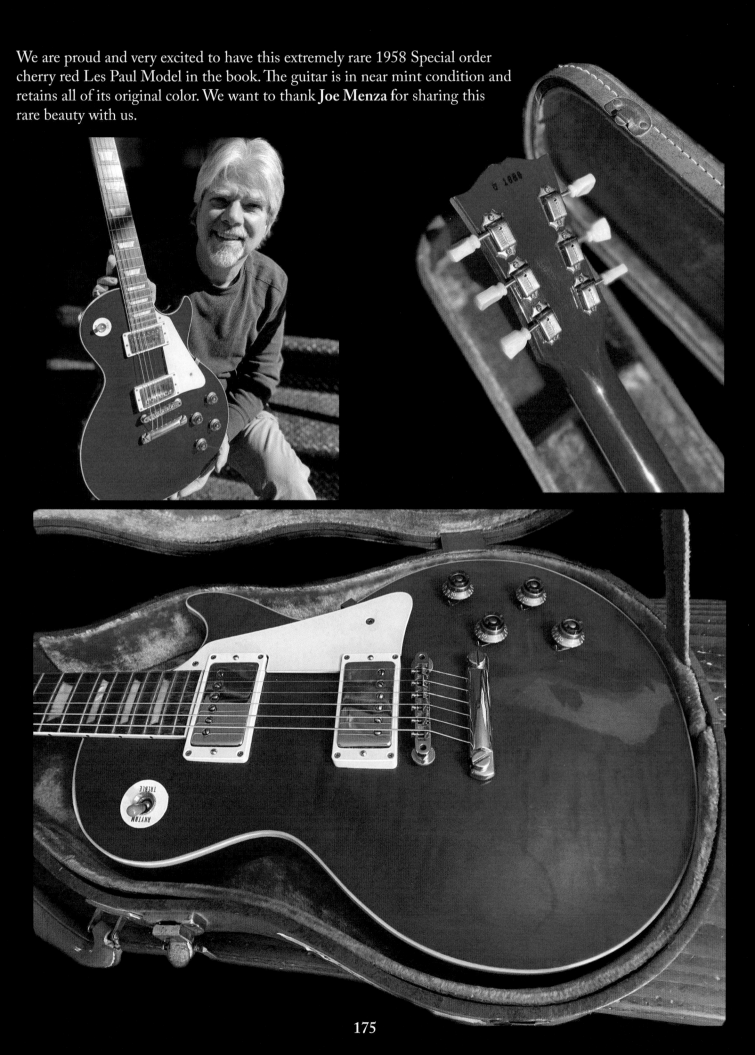

175

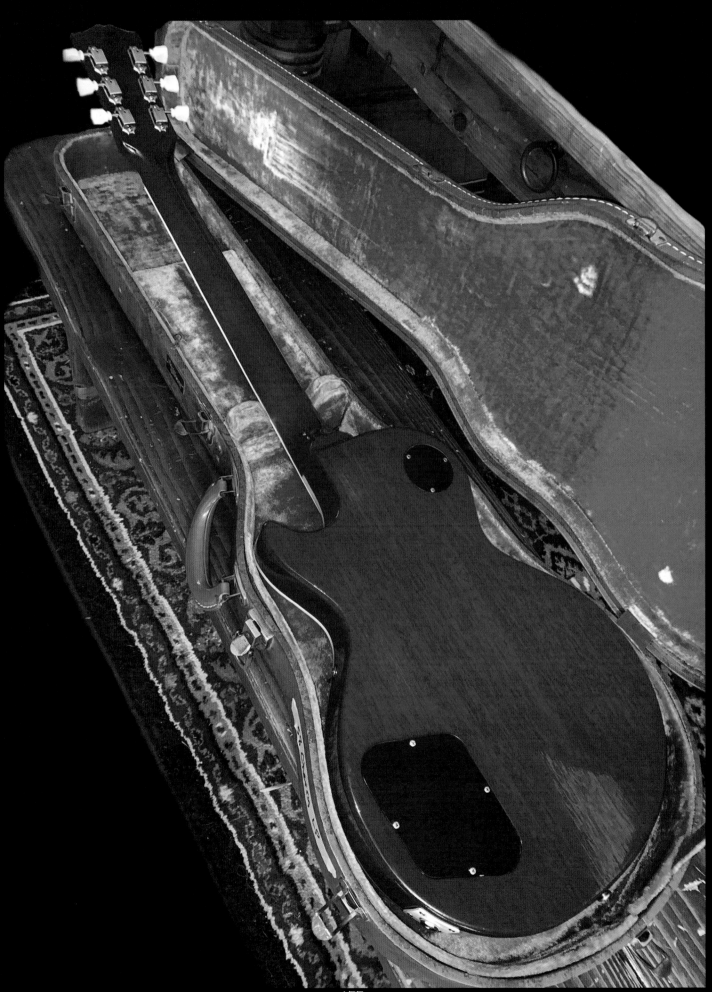

8 2793
'GoldenEye'

The shaded area near the selector was
caused by the original tag

Mono-Plak attached to the
CaliGirl case.

Photo credit: Roberto Gandolfi

8 3324

This Les Paul with the flowered armrest and pickguard was specially made for Mary Ford.

8 3832 'Oscar'

Courtesy of Doug and Pat

8 3967

belonged to a local guitarist in the band Pezband, whose two guitarists played 58 standards, one Gold, one Burst. They were the band every guitar geek wanted to see. When he found a 59 Burst he sold the Goldtop in 74-5 and it wound up with Paul Hamer, who owned Northern Prairie Music, one of the first vintage guitar shops, and then, later Hamer Guitars.

Thanks to Barry Gold

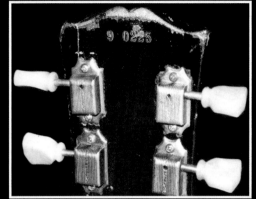

We apologize for the terrible quality of the photo, but this is quite an important guitar in the Goldtop series. By mid 1958, the new cherry sunburst finish Les Paul's were introduced and the gold finish was discontinued. This particular Les Paul # 9 0225 was the last Goldtop produced. Maybe it was a 'leftover' 1958 that was sitting around the factory and shipped in early 1959 or a special order for a customer who didn't like the new sunburst finish We'll never really know.

Thank you, Julio, for your burstserial.com site that lets us have an instant view of so many great and rare Les Pauls.

The Rolling Stones – Goldtops

Although Brian Jones was primarily associated with the Vox Mark Teardrop shaped guitar and both reverse and non reverse Gibson Firebird VII's, he is shown here playing the recently introduced 1968 Gibson Goldtop. Brian is seen in the classic 1968 movie, Rock&Roll Circus with this newly released Les Paul Standard.

thanks to Eliot Easton for these two photos

Eliot Easton

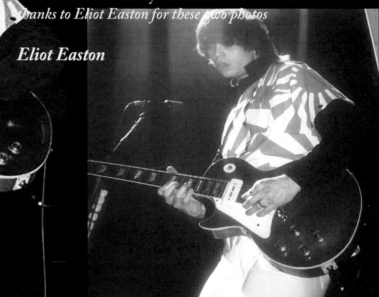

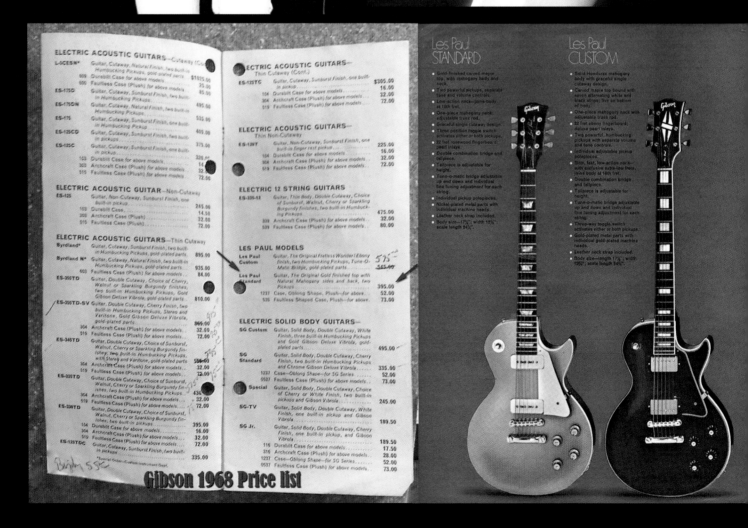

Gibson 1968 Price list

184

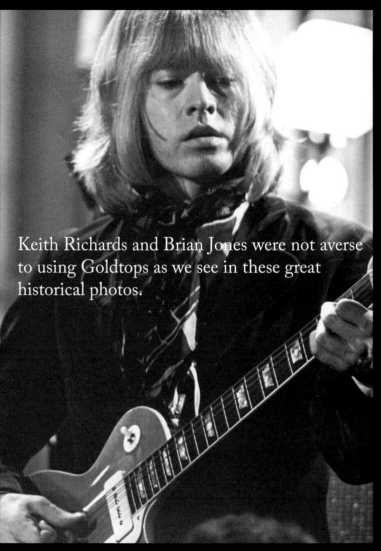

Keith Richards and Brian Jones were not averse to using Goldtops as we see in these great historical photos.

Keith and Etta James at The Bitter End, New York 1982 playing Brian Ray's Goldtop.
Photo courtesy of Brian Ray

Les Dudek pt 1. the Allman Brothers, Boz Scaggs and Steve Miller

1968 'Alma'

Named after his mom and a great studio photo from 1969 with the guitar in its original state

Hi everybody, Les Dudek here,
So Vic Dapra reached out to me and asked if I'd like to be in his book about Gibson Goldtop Les Paul guitars. Apparently, Vic remembered me from the 70s, when I released two of my solo albums on Columbia Records, that featured two different Gibson Goldtop Les Pauls on the front covers. My first solo record "Les Dudek" (debut) is the one with a large Scarlett Macaw parrot perched on the guitar neck, that Goldtop is my 1968. And the guitar pictured on my second album "Say No More" with my friend Angela Caprie, (Telly "Kojak" Savalas' niece) pouring champagne that is defying gravity, is my 1956 Goldtop.

By the time the 60s came around I had already owned a few guitars, my first electric was a Silvertone 1446L Premier. Then my '65 Ventures model Mosrite. I also owned a red Gibson SG with two P-90s, like the one Carlos Santana used in the Woodstock movie. At the end of the 60s, I recall it was the end of November 1968, I went to my local music store, (Carlton Music) Winter Haven, Florida. Our local music store that senior peers of mine, Jim Stafford (I Don't Like Spiders & Snakes) and Gram Parsons (The Birds) also frequented. Gibson had just re-released the original style Les Paul models again in 1968. As we all know, Gibson stopped making the original style Les Pauls from '61 to '68. That's when they used the Les Paul name on their new SG models, (Les Paul wasn't happy about that). But they came back out with the original style Les Paul again in 1968. There they were hanging on the wall. Carlton Music just received a black Les Paul Custom, and a Goldtop Les Paul Standard. I fell in love with the Goldtop. My Mom and Dad said OK son, we'll buy you the Goldtop, but that's the last guitar we're buying you, you're on your own after this. Consequently, that Goldtop has been with me throughout my entire career in music, and is today, my most prized guitar. Thanks again Mom & Dad, my 68 Goldtop is still a constant reminder of your love.

I call my 1968 Goldtop 'Alma', I named her after my Mom's first name. Although Mom and Dad both bought me the guitar, it was Mom who truly understood my love for playing the guitar. Mom was from Brooklyn, New York, she also had a love for show biz. In her youth, she would moonlight with a dance team called the Rockettes. Her brother, my uncle Joe, had a long-running comedy burlesque show called "Bottoms Up", based in Las Vegas. Show biz was in the blood.

Alma went through several morphs over the years. At first she had all the cream colored trim (P-90 pickup covers, pickguard, the round plate for the toggle switch, and the plate for the plug in jack. Please refer to my first picture with Alma in this article, taken in 1969. Shortly after, I decided to change all the cream colored trim to black, and I changed out the tuning pegs to Grover's. Then in the late '70s after installing EMGs in my 1972 Strat, I found the EMGs to be completely quiet of noise in the studio. So I decided to change out the P-90 pickups in Alma to a set of EMG's with a pre-amp. The EMG pickups are hot, and sound dangerously great, they have no noise hum of any kind, so they are fabulous for recording in the studio. My only major complaint is, the guy who installed the EMGs, (John Carruthers) drilled a hole in the face of Alma to install an on/off toggle switch for the pre-amp, (without even asking me first). After all these years, I still would like to strangle him for doing that. He could have used a push pull pot on one of the tone pots, for the pre-amp on/off switch, without ever drilling a hole in the face of Alma. I can't express into words how pissed off I am at him for doing that. I still have all the original pickup, covers and trim, and at one point wanted to change her back to original, but can't because of the hole that was drilled in my guitar.

'Alma' today

I don't ever plan on selling Alma, and she sounds so good, I decided to clean her up, and keep her the way she is. Billy Fels in Orlando (Guitar Factory) repaired a fret inlay, and new pick up rings. He also advised me to leave her the way she is, don't repair the hole. Please refer to the current pictures of Alma. I only use Alma in the studio and never take her out. Alma has a resume full of music history, for posterity sake, I retired her from the road. She has paid her dues. There are a few places on earth that I know would love to have her on display. One of those places is the Allman Brothers Band Big House Museum, in Macon, Georgia. The next paragraph will give you more history about why Alma has earned her place in the ABB Museum.

Les Dudek pt2. the Allman Brothers, Boz Scaggs and Steve Miller

As I mentioned previously, Alma made her visual appearance on my first Columbia Records solo (debut) album cover, titled Les Dudek. Or as the French would call it, "The Dudek." There's another quick story I'll tell you about my name. My dear old friend Leon Wilkeson (R.I.P.) bass player in Lynyrd Skynyrd, dubbed me, "The Dude, with a special K", (that was for you Leon). All right, back to Alma. Before Alma's visual appearance, the reason why the ABB Museum in Macon, GA would most likely love to display Alma, is because she made her first audio appearance on, The Allman Brothers Band's biggest hit single, "Ramblin' Man", from the (Brothers & Sisters album), Capricorn Records 1973. That's Alma and me playing all those guitar harmonies with Dickey Betts. Alma became a star, on a #1 hit. In the two and a half years I lived in the ABB camp, Alma was used at many jams, with the boys from Wet Willy, Marshall Tucker and so many others. Pictured here on my birthday 1973 Alma & I are jamming with Greg Allman (R.I.P.) at Grants Lounge Macon, GA.

Allman and Dudek 1973

**Dudek & Scaggs Guitar Player Mag
May '76 my '68 Goldtop**

While I lived in Macon, GA, my manager then, Phil Walden, hooked me up with Boz Scaggs, who was on the road at the time, desperate to find another guitar player to replace the one he just fired. Alma & I flew to Akron, Ohio and got the gig with Boz. The next five and a half years Alma & I played for Scaggs. Here I supplied concert pictures of Alma and me with Boz. Alma is also the guitar I used in all the original videos from Boz's Silk Degrees films, (Low Down, Lido and the others). Alma can also be heard on Boz's Silk Degees album, I used her to play slide guitar on the song "Jump Street." In 1974, while on the road with Boz, Alma and I did a long run with The Steve Miller Band, supporting his "Joker" hit. At the end of that run, Miller invited Alma and me to do some recording with him in Seattle, WA. From those recordings, you can hear Alma on Steve Miller's, Fly Like An Eagle, Book Of Dreams, and Living In The Twentieth Century Albums. In 1975 Miller invited me to play a festival with him at Knebworth Park, England, with Pink Floyd. Miller mentioned on Jimmy Fallon's, The Tonight Show, it was the biggest show attendance he ever played to. And there was Alma and me, playing "Rockin' Me Babe" for the very first time in front of an audience of 120,000 people.

And the story goes on and on about Alma, from using her when I worked with Stevie Nicks, Steppin Wolf, the very first Journey rehearsal, (that's a whole other story), all the way to working with Cher. Alma has been with me the whole time. And I made sure Alma always appears on all my records. Most recently Alma appears on most of the solo work from my latest "Delta Breeze" CD.

Dudek & Nicks 1991

Boz and Dudek 1970's with his 1968 Goldtop "Alma"

Then we have my 1956 Goldtop, of which, unfortunately, has a much shorter history, and stay with me. My 1956 Goldtop was pictured on my second album cover titled "Say No More", Columbia Records. And here I am in 1977, white suit and all, with my 1956 Goldtop in a promo pic for that album. I kept the cream colored trim on the '56. The sad note is, the 56 was stolen November 1979. I'm still sick about that. The good news is, they didn't get Alma, my '68. I used my '56 Goldtop on parts of my, "Say No More", "Ghost Town Parade", and "DFK" albums before she was abducted. I also had an original 1961 red SG stolen with the '56 Goldtop.

I was never a guitar hoarder, I didn't have a place to keep them. So I only had the guitars I needed, I was done buying electric guitars. I owned a Gibson 1968 & 1956 Goldtop Les Paul, a 1961 SG, and a Fender 1972 Strat. For the kind of music I played, they worked for me. Then the '61 SG and '56 Goldtop were both stolen, a very sad day indeed.

1977 promo photo with 1956 Goldtop

Les Dudek pt3. the Allman Brothers, Boz Scaggs and Steve Miller

Berkley Community Theater 1973 with "Alma"
Photo Credit: Jim Marshall

Here's a story about Gibson I'll share with you. I went to Gibson a few years after my 61 SG & 56 Goldtop were stolen. I asked Gibson if they could please do me a mercy deal, something, throw me a bone. I needed to replace those two Gibsons that I loved and used religiously. They asked me, what have I done for them? I replied I think I may have helped sell at least a few truckloads of Goldtop Les Pauls for you. After displaying two Gibson Goldtops on the front cover) of two of my major Columbia Records releases. Of which, also got all kinds of press, in all the big music magazines from Rolling Stone on. So I thought, just maybe Gibson would remember that I already did a lot for them. So please, can you help me replace two of my beloved Gibson guitars.

Gibson refused to do anything for me, they gave me the manufacturing dime tour in Nashville instead. At the end of the tour, I spotted about a 25 foot rack of Les Pauls. I asked, what are you doing with these guitars? They said those are slated for demolition. I picked up one to look at it, I played it, couldn't find anything wrong with it. They said it has a little nick on the binding. I asked, can you work with me on this one, they replied, no can do, we must destroy all these guitars.

Steve Miller Band Knebworth England 1975 with "Alma."

That was the day I stopped playing Gibson. After all the press I generated for their guitars, they would rather destroy a guitar with a nick than work a deal with me. I've had many, many fans ask me over the years, why I stopped playing Gibson Les Pauls, well, now you know why.

That was many years ago, and since then, I finely broke down and bought two 61 re-issue Custom Shop SGs to replace my stolen original 1961 SG. If anyone at Gibson is reading this, I would still like to replace the Les Paul that was stolen. A 1960 reissue, slim neck cherry/tiger Sunburst from the Gibson Custom Shop would be my choice...Hello Gibson, I'm not hard to find if you ever have a change of heart. www.lesdudek.com

Thank you, Vic, for asking me to share my Gibson Goldtop stories with you and your readers. Of course, I have many more stories about Alma, but I'll save those for my book, if I ever get around to writing it. Good luck to all you guitar pickers out there. And, LONG LIVE THE BLUES!!

Les

1968
506138

An early '68 with unusual "Crown" headstock and '67 pots

Photo credit Phil Carwardine
philsvintageguitars.com

1968
522819

1968 Les Paul Standard. Here is a pristine example. When introduced, this was Gibson's first "Reissue" Les Paul guitar, along with the LP Custom model that shortly followed. It was not officially dubbed a "reissue," but was intended to be a recreation of the 1956 P-90 "Standard" model. This guitar marked the reentry of the Solid-body, Single cut-away Les Paul guitar back into the product lineup after being absent for about 7 years. The earlier examples have 1 piece mahogany neck construction and the correct small headstock shape, reminiscent of the original 1956 guitars. Subsequently, after the early production runs ended, Gibson decided to modify the features and these guitars quickly received the same large headstock and 3 piece Mahogany necks as the other production instruments of the Norlin era. There was also a brief, short-lived "transitional" version that featured a larger headstock and 1-piece neck. The earlier small head and 1 piece neck guitars have full and round feeling neck profiles with 1 11/16" nut widths. Luckily, this model didn't receive the narrowed nut spec of the majority of the late 1960s period instruments, making these some of the more desirable and valuable guitars of this period. Despite the description in the 1968 Catalog, these guitars were not issued with Nickel-plated parts as Chrome plating was instead used. It was quite common in the 1960s for guitar manufacturers to release new catalogs but display earlier instruments and/or erroneous spec information, so the catalog images and or listed specifications could not always be relied upon at the time of printing, which usually pre-dated the actual release of the instruments. The 1968 model Goldtops with the early features are "Reissue" guitars, the later, large headstock models cannot be considered Reissues as their construction dramatically differs from the 1956 models they were intended to mimic.

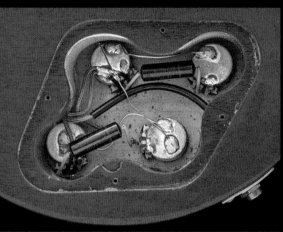

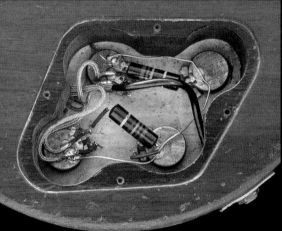

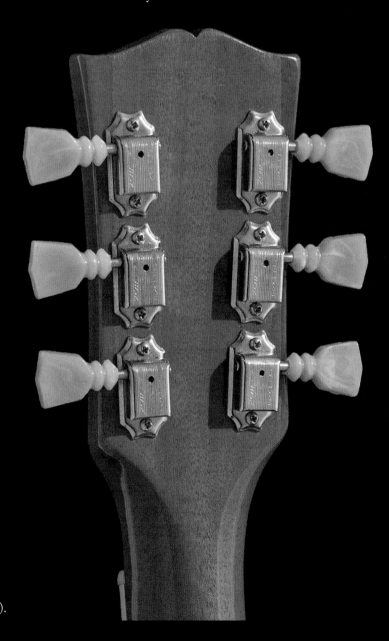

There is an old wives tale that's circulated for decades, so please note that NONE of these reissued Goldtops are made with left-over bodies or necks from the 1950's. A quick comparison of the 1968 control cavity (top) reveals construction differences compared to a 1959 (below).

Photos and Feature by Albert Molinaro

1968 Les Paul Standard

Here is a rare and pristine "Dark Back" example from 1968. The dark back finish was applied to many P-90 and Humbucking Standard models dating back to the mid 1950s. Many Les Pauls were finished this way up through 1958, but few 1968 examples have been found.

The Rhythm / Treble ring exhibits the same typeface as the late 1950's Les Pauls utilized.

Here you can see that the 1968 models have a "thick" binding in the cutaway, another feature that separates them from the original 1950's models.

Photos and Feature by Albert Molinaro

541741
1969

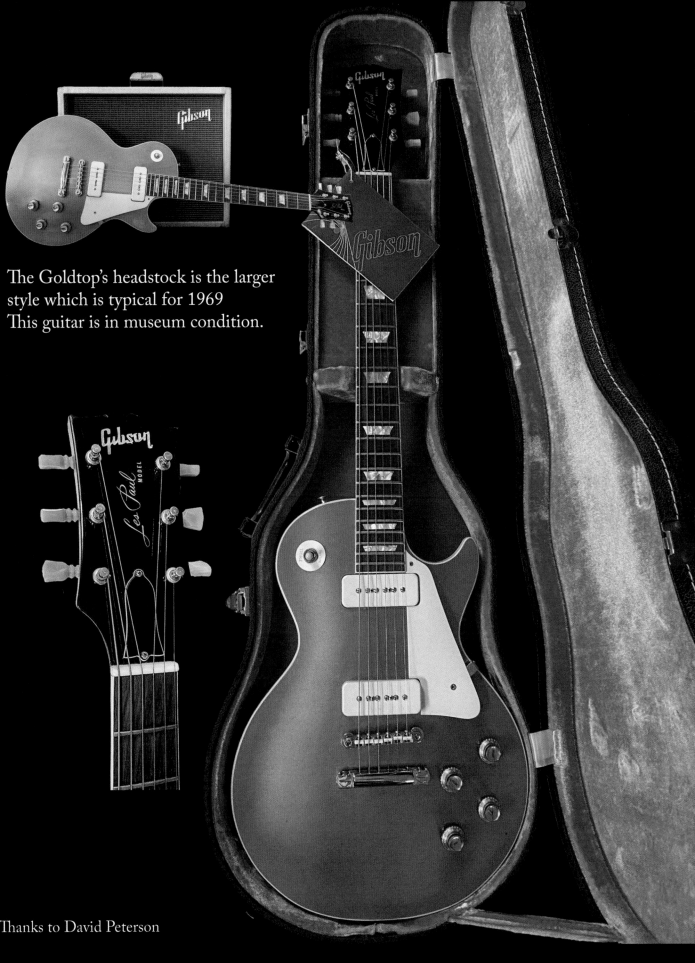

The Goldtop's headstock is the larger
style which is typical for 1969
This guitar is in museum condition.

Thanks to David Peterson

551859

1969

558337

1969

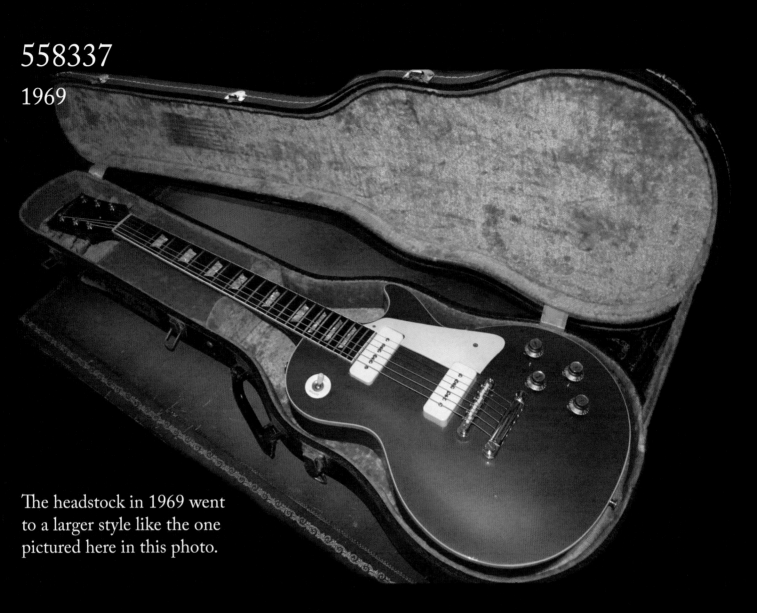

The headstock in 1969 went to a larger style like the one pictured here in this photo.

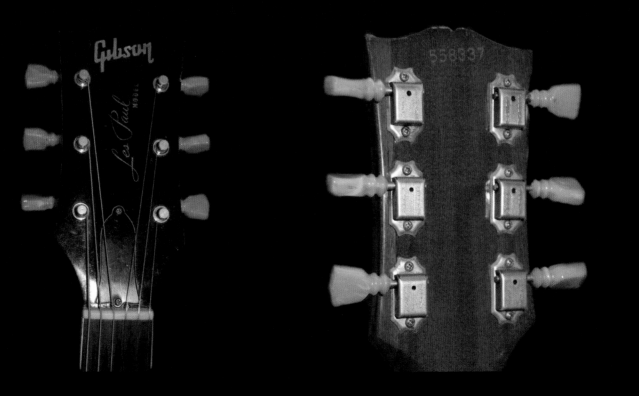

Some great images of an early 1969
Gibson Les Paul Standard. The
guitar has a one piece neck, one piece
body, no volute and the pots date to
the first week of 1969.

RHYTHM TREBLE

Photo Credit: ReCaster

Stan Webb

Photo credit: Lynne Weller

803205

Here's a great photo of Stan Webb from Chicken Shack with his late '60s Goldtop showing honest playing wear.

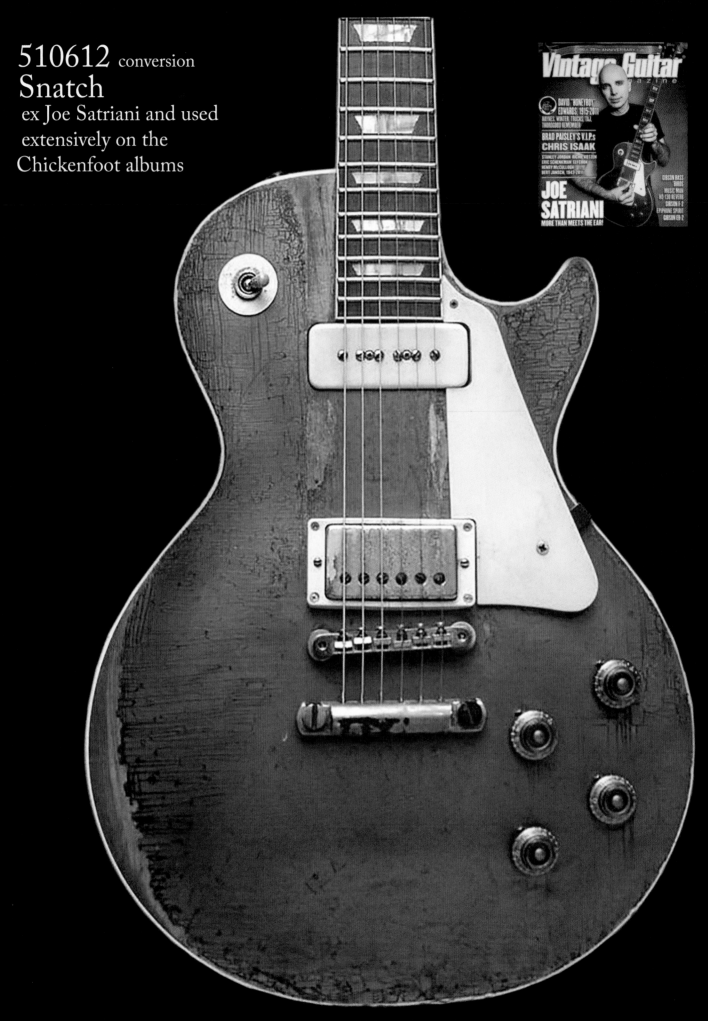

510612 conversion
Snatch
ex Joe Satriani and used
extensively on the
Chickenfoot albums

1953 - 1954
Conversion

This Goltop had already been converted when I bought it. It had an ambered opaque finish on the top that needed some correction and a fret job. The top is original wood. The back and neck were fine and did not require any work.

JamesMassey

Photo credit: Carter Vintage Guitars

1955/57
conversion

An example of a good conversion and a guitar which **Bernie Marsden** often takes to studio sesssion as it is a great sounding instrument.

Tom Scholz

Tom Scholz's reputation as a technological wizard and gear-hound is well deserved, as the Boston guitarist holds enough electronics-related patents to wallpaper his home studio. That being the case, you might surmise the veteran player owns a commensurate number of electric guitars. In fact, nothing could be further from the truth. "I have only two guitars," Scholz says. "They're both old Les Paul Goldtops. I bought them both used, at a time when I didn't know anything about Les Pauls. Somebody told me that these two guitars were made for only six months — during half of 1968 — so there are only a very few in existence. The neck on the guitar is completely different from the neck on every other type of Les Paul. It's huge. At first I couldn't play on it at all, and then after finally learning how to play on it, I discovered that there weren't any others available. But the amazing thing is I found two of them, without knowing that the second one was from 1968 as well, from that six-month period. This happened before the first Boston album was released. I needed a second guitar before we went on the road, so I snatched it up. I bought both guitars for about $300."

614032
1956

The guitar was heavily
modified at one point and brought
back to its original specs.

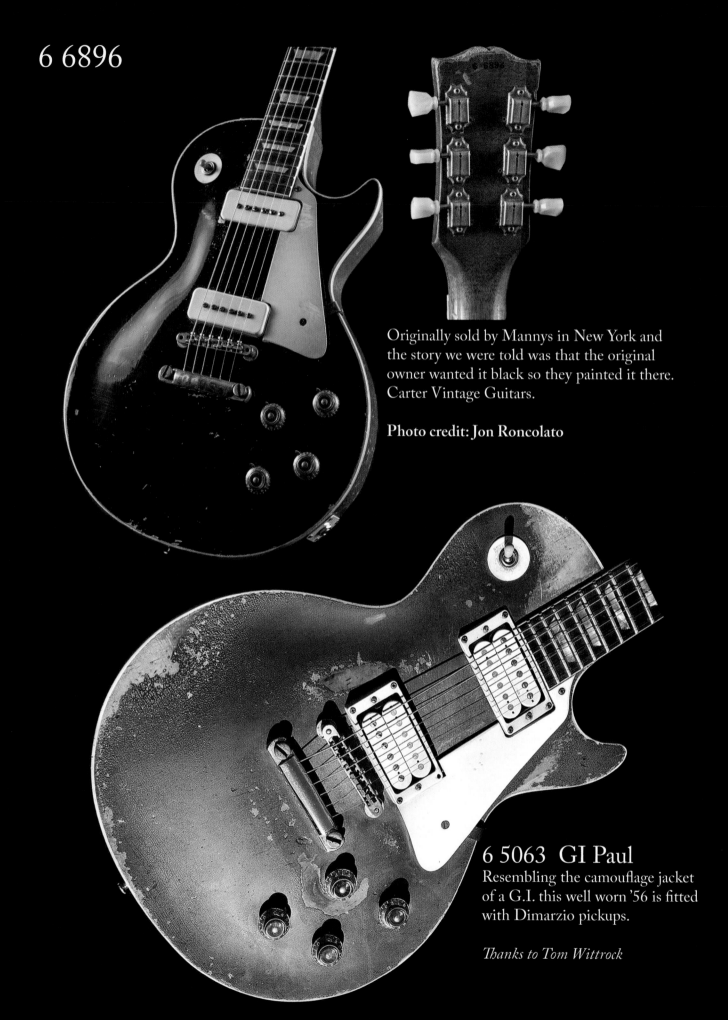

6 6896

Originally sold by Mannys in New York and
the story we were told was that the original
owner wanted it black so they painted it there.
Carter Vintage Guitars.

Photo credit: Jon Roncolato

6 5063 GI Paul
Resembling the camouflage jacket
of a G.I. this well worn '56 is fitted
with Dimarzio pickups.

Thanks to Tom Wittrock

A '53 conversion
from Yukki Mcclure

Nicknamed 'Soul Patch' this guitar started life as a 1953 trapeze tailpiece Les Paul. It was sent back to Gibson in 1963 for a total refin and new neck as the original neck was broken. Gibson doesn't repair necks, they replace them. A cherry sunburst was added, humbucking pickups, tune-o-matic bridge and a 1960s style trapeze tailpiece A stop tailpiece was added much later down the road. You can still see the shadow where the 60's tailpiece was located. Fitted with Creamtone parts.

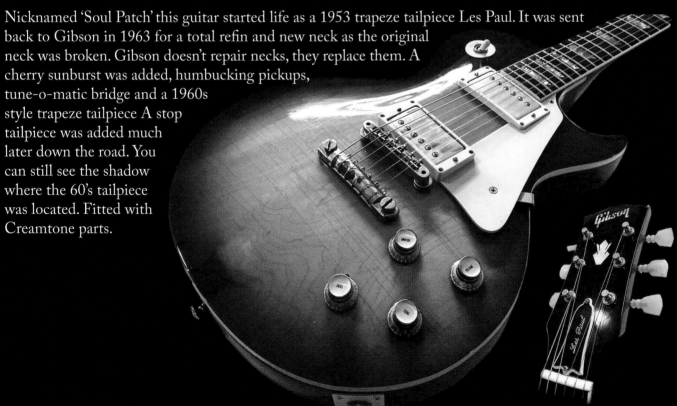

This recent photo is a reminder of the life
and times during the Covid 19 pandemic

Mike Campbell

We close with this great Live shot of Mike and Tom. Although 1971 is just beyond the book's time-line parameter, Mike's 1971 Limited Edition is worthy of inclusion. Mike is a veteran member of the music world and a creative player and artist with an enviable career.
Mike generously responds to requests to participate in the books with photos and quotes.
We are truly grateful for the efforts that all of the book's contributors have made.

Below Photo: The Old Waldorf Nightclub, San Francisco, California, circa 1977
Photo by Richard McCaffrey/ Michael Ochs Archive Getty Images

"…back in Florida, I had previously been using mostly Fenders and had been playing a Strat, although I did have a 3 pickup Red Firebird, which sounded bright to me and I always wanted a thicker sounding Gibson.

While recording the first record, I went down to Nadine's Music in Hollywood and they showed me the Goldtop along with a Broadcaster, which I didn't know much about at that time but also still have, and I liked and bought them BOTH on a whim that day.
When they first showed me the Les Paul, I thought the pickups were custom made models, although I did learn soon after that only the cream plastic covers had been removed, revealing the bobbins and coils.

I used the guitar on a bunch of the early records and it stayed with us. I also played it on the Mudcrutch record we did too. Thinking back, I remember that Tom played the rhythm tracks on "Mary Jane's Last Dance" with this Les Paul.

I've always loved the   jfinish and have coveted the look of them."

Photos and feature courtesy of Albert Molinaro

Mike's 1971 Limited Edition "1958 Les Paul"

The 1971 reissue guitars have 1 piece non-laminated bodies and thin binding in the cutaway

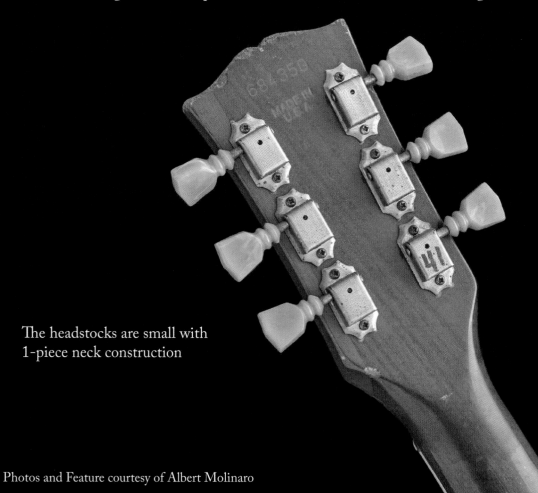

The headstocks are small with
1-piece neck construction

Goldtop

Believers

Gallery

8 3668
Mike Reeder

610786 Phil Carwardine

1952
Francesco
Balossino

7 0733
Mike Slubowski

1953

Gruhn-Guitars

1952
Adam White

8 1791
Ed Snape

7 3317 Clive Kay

7 6186 Alan Grace

Christian Bohnert 1952 1957

614715 Ed Snape

612333 Hiroshi Inoue

1952 Andrea Cesarini

7 1390
John Coleman

8 3129 Vince Sobocinski

4 2160 Eirik Jaer

4 1134 Peter Kriemler

5 6990 Don Lee

Flame top clearly seen through
the gold finish. Alan Grace

52   5 2   5 3   53   5 3

Greg Platza

541741
Dave Peterson

4 3684
Bob Wooton

219

Goldtop
Believers
Gallery

4 1738 Marco Gerber

7 3742 Paul Dee

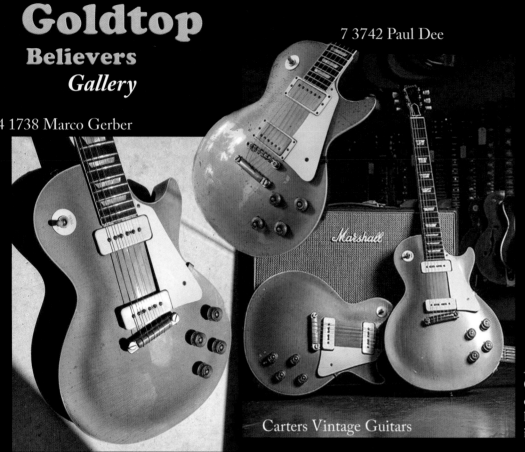

850145

Carters Vintage Guitars

According to Mike Reeder this Goldtop is a 1969. Could be one of the first GT's to have mini humbuckers – possibly shipped in 1970

1952 Marco Gerber

532039
Paul Beck

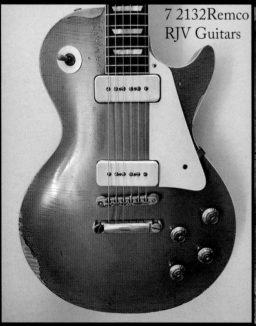

7 2132 Remco
RJV Guitars

3 1837 Dag Luyten & 4 1637 Vasco Rosin

1956 Kepha

6 1280
Rob Doolittle

Bill Fajen
4 2850 7 3762

6 5954
Alan Grace

8 1144
burstserial.com

1952 Matt King

8 2794
Tim Erringtonn

8 1793 top
8 3127 bottom
Bill Fajen

An early 1950s ad for the Gibson Les Paul. Note the heavily modified guitars Les and Mary are playing. Both of these instruments are far from the stock model which makes one wonder if Les was happy with his new namesake guitar.

THEY'RE TOPS... LES PAUL, MARY FORD AND THEIR GIBSONS

Gibson Inc.,
Kalamazoo, Mich.

Its wondrous tone, unique features and beautiful styling have recorded a hit from coast to coast for the Les Paul Model. Guitarists marvel at the new design and playing ease, listeners enthuse over the exciting tonal qualities and sharp contrasts. Like its designer, the Gibson Les Paul Model is "star quality" in every respect.

The Grande Finale

And so we come to the end of Goldtop Believers and what a blast it has been – this edition caught the imagination of the Goldtop owners who had felt sidelined with the Burst series but now were given the opportunity to show off their revered GT's. We also introduced quite a few renowned Goldtops artists who were new to the series. Once again we had terrific support from all levels of players with the usual high standard of photography.

Thanks to each and every one of you.

Vic and David

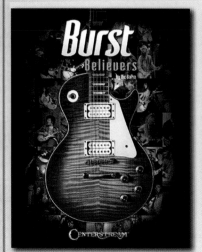
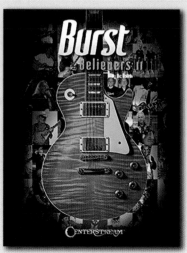
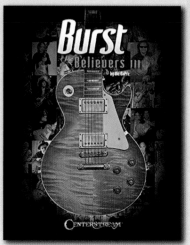
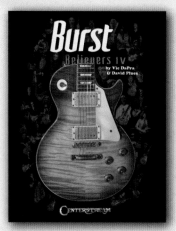